JAMIE DURIE'S

EDIBLE

GARDEN

DESIGN

BENEFITS OF AN EDIBLE GARDEN

GROWING YOUR OWN EDIBLES WILL BENEFIT YOUR BODY, YOUR MIND, YOUR SPIRIT, YOUR TASTEBUDS, YOUR KIDS, YOUR WALLET, AND THE ENVIRONMENT.

HERE'S HOW:

- You will know that the food you are eating is free from harmful pesticides and has not been genetically modified.

- The food you grow yourself always tastes so much better than anything you buy.

- You will lower your carbon footprint and decrease food miles.

- You will spend quality time with your kids, teaching them the importance of growing things and being connected to nature and its cycles.

- Gardening is good exercise.

- Eating what you grow will help you stay healthy and give you a great sense of well-being.

- You will save money since you won't need to buy as much, because you'll be supplementing your diet with food straight out of your backyard.

- You will feel a great sense of pride and satisfaction from providing food for yourself and your family.

- Your gratitude to Mother Nature for her ability to provide food will make you love nature even more, and you will be less wasteful with food when you are growing it yourself—it's a win for the planet and also for you.

JAMIE DURIE'S

EDIBLE

GARDEN

DESIGN

HARPER DESIGN

An Imprint of HarperCollins Publishers

CONTENTS

INTRODUCTION

There has never been a more exciting time to start an edible garden. Vertical, stackable, curbside, rooftop, community, windowsill, recycled… The fruit and veggie patch is getting a makeover and, as a result, our cities are too.

The global movement toward a more sustainable future has become a part of our everyday life, whether you live in the city, the suburbs, or the country. It's no longer a question of whether you can help, but how you can do it. People across the globe are reinventing, recycling, and reinvigorating the way they live, creating a healthier future for the planet and generations to come.

A well-loved garden has a wonderful way of nurturing you, providing a sense of sanctuary and joy—when you add edible plants it becomes holistic, a garden you can truly interact with. What could be better than a productive garden that is as beautiful as it is functional?

How many times have you vowed to start growing your own edibles, but not known how or where to start? Or thought it was all too hard because you live in the city with little or no garden space? Or been put off because you thought it would cost a fortune? If this sounds like you, keep reading.

Here you will find delicious design ideas that you can adapt to suit your own space and lifestyle. I am so grateful to the many visionary gardeners, communities, architects, chefs, and individuals from all over the world who have generously shared the stories of their gardens. Read about them and be inspired, as I have been.

I can't wait to share with you my edible design philosophy, which is the product of three decades of landscape design experience, plus ideas I have collected from my travels. Whether you live in an apartment building, in a rental home, by yourself, or with a large family, this book will point you in the right direction and offer solutions to growing your own edibles, that look great, no matter where or how you live.

I hope this book will inspire you to design your own edible utopia. Embrace it, share it, and get started!

Yumie

CHAPTER ONE

DELICIOUS DESIGN

Connect your space inside and out, then integrate edible plants you can grow, smell, touch, eat, and share. With a few simple guidelines you can design an edible garden that not only tastes delicious but also looks incredible.

THE OUTDOOR ROOM PHILOSOPHY

Before I get to my "Delicious Design Philosophy" for creating edible yet beautifully designed gardens that suit your lifestyle, I want to touch on my general philosophy for designing gardens, since this is where the idea was born. I call it "The Outdoor Room Philosophy," and it's all about creating gardens for people to live in, not just to look at from the kitchen window. Your garden, whether it's a backyard or a balcony, should be about lounging, dining, cooking, or bathing—or the whole lot. Think of turning your house inside out and expanding all your favorite rooms into the outdoors. Give your outdoor space a more meaningful purpose and make it a true extension of your home—think of it as your new (outdoor) room. It's about "Destination Design"—build it and they will come. By creating spaces that people relate to, where they will want to spend time, they will automatically reconnect with nature and stay awhile. . .

The success of a garden depends entirely on how it makes people feel. I'm passionate about creating what I call "The Human Garden" or "people-pockets"—spaces where people want to spend time. Great gardens are not just about grand gestures—they're about the details that turn an ornamental garden into a human space, encouraging people to interact with them by creating a sense of comfort, by architecturally inviting or even seducing people into the great outdoors. Creating human spaces comes down to making destinations that draw people outside. It's about intelligent, intuitive design that recognizes the way we interact socially, and the way we relax and unwind.

Here are some things to consider:

DELICIOUS
DESIGN—
WHERE IT
ALL BEGAN

- **Conversation corners:** Incorporate plenty of different seating nooks in your garden. When people are relaxed they spontaneously converse. Think about the purpose of each seat: do you want to have a quiet chat with a loved one? If so, an L-shape or even C-shape help conversation, since they encourage eye contact. Or do you want a daybed you can relax on? First consider how you want to use the garden, then design it around that.

- **Dual purpose:** I'm always looking for an opportunity to turn a retaining wall, a fence, or a corner into a seating area. If your garden bed edges are wide enough (between 12 to 16 inches), they automatically become a place to sit. If the change of level within the garden is around 11 to 20 inches, that's another opportunity to incorporate seating-width retaining walls, inviting people to stay awhile. There's nothing like sitting in a sunken lounge area, surrounded by lush greenery.

- **Destination design:** Do you want your friends to be able to gather round and share a meal, lounge around an open fire at night, cook outside in a kitchen that feels like it should be inside? Do you want a quiet nook for yourself where you can just meditate or read? You can create all these destinations, and more, through clever design.

- **Garden magnets:** Use focal points to draw people outside—you might choose a beautiful sculpture or a spectacular accent plant. Once people are in the garden, make sure there is plenty to encourage them to stay; take them on a journey and create a sense of intrigue and discovery.

- **Create warmth:** To get the most out of your outdoor room in the cooler months, install a fire pit. Humans have an almost primal attraction to fire and it is a wonderful way to encourage conversation and connection.

LUXESCAPING

Another part of my garden design philosophy, and something that I am particularly passionate about, is infusing a sense of luxury into every single garden I design. I call it luxescaping. Luxescaping is about luxury and functionality in equal measure, not just about creating expensive gardens. Everyday comforts suddenly become special when created outdoors. Showering outside among ferns and palm trees sounds pretty enticing, right? Cooking suddenly becomes more fun, and everything tastes better outside. Everyone wants to feel nurtured, especially if it is by nature.

If you want to luxescape your backyard, think about the things you love doing the most at home. Do you love reading? How about creating a reading nook in your backyard, with comfortable outdoor fabric cushions, protected from harsh midday sun, wind or rain? Or if you love lying in the bath, consider installing an outdoor bathtub, surrounded by screen planting to ensure complete privacy. I did, and it is amazing!

Luxescaping your existing garden may be as simple as updating the furnishings. These days there is a huge range of fabulous outdoor fabrics you can use for cushions and lounges and even as curtains in your garden. Adding lighting is another simple way to luxescape your garden. Use lights to define different spaces, create ambience, and draw people outside at night. Hang a chandelier over your outdoor dining table or uplight the elegant bare branches of a cherry or apple tree. Lighting can really make a space feel special! Not to mention the fact that you get a twenty-four-hour garden instead of a twelve-hour one—double the use and impact.

EDIBLE GARDENS

My philosophy with edible gardens is exactly the same. The more liveable they are, the more time you'll spend in them and the more you'll value them. The more you value them, the more effort and creativity you will give them. It's simple—we nurture nature, and nature nurtures us.

There are some extra challenges with edibles because you are choosing plants for their produce, whereas garden designers typically choose plants for their shape, texture, and density. So, to create a successful edible garden where you can entertain, cook, or simply lounge about, choose plants that provide the food you crave and the function you need. When you grow food you are creating an interactive garden. It is a true labor of love—the more you put in, the more you get out.

Many fruit, vegetables, and herbs are seasonal, so to create garden beds that look good all year round, you need to rely on plants that I call the bones of the design: steadfast evergreens and perennials that add structure, form, and frame to the edibles, which are replanted from season to season. These more structural plants give your garden design the consistency it needs so you can give the sometimes unruly edibles the freedom they need to thrive.

To design with edibles you need to change your perception; don't just look at the plant for its food value, consider its ornamental value as well. Shape, habit, color, texture, density—this is the way designers choose their palette.

You'll soon discover there is an edible plant out there to perform almost every design trick in the book. Your edible garden will look every bit as sexy as your neighbors' purely ornamental gardens—only you get a harvest of fresh food as a bonus.

GETTING CREATIVE WITH EDIBLES

The more I garden, the more I learn. I have now built up a library of plants in my head that I know I can rely on when I design a garden.

Here are some ways I have used edibles over the years: bay trees or pomegranate for screens, rosemary for hedging, parsley and sage for borders, apples and pears for raised pleached (entwined) aerial hedges, dill and parsnip for fine foliage movement in the garden, artichokes for accent, pumpkins for ground covers, grapes and passion fruit for trellises and walls, fig trees for shady canopies or garden ceilings, citrus and stone fruits for topiary ornamental trees.

VITAMINS AND MINERALS

B

asparagus
avocado
banana
broccoli
cauliflower
corn

leafy greens
mushrooms
passion fruit
peas
potato
sweet potato

C

asparagus
blueberries
broccoli
Brussels sprouts
cabbage
capsicum
cauliflower
grapefruit
guava
kiwifruit
leafy greens

lemon
mango
orange
parsley
pawpaw
peas
strawberries
tomato

A

apricot
capsicum
carrot
dark leafy greens
green beans
mango
peas
pumpkin
sweet potato
tomato
yellow peaches

E

avocado
blackberry
corn
mango
parsnips
pear

plum
pumpkin
raspberry
spinach
sweet potato
tomato

D

gardening in
the sunshine!

CALCIUM

almonds
brazil nuts
broccoli
leafy greens
watercress

K

asparagus
broccoli
Brussels sprouts
carrot
cucumber
dark leafy greens
lettuce
peas
spring onion

MAGNESIUM

almonds
apple
apricot
artichoke
avocado
banana
Brussels sprouts
corn

cucumber
grapefruit
leafy greens
pawpaw
peas
pumpkin
sweet potato

ZINC

leafy greens
nuts
pumpkin seeds

IRON

apricot
cabbage
leafy greens
pumpkin seeds

Not everyone has the luxury of building the edible utopia of their dreams, but if you choose the right style of garden to suit your needs, your garden (and you!) will thrive. In this section, I talk about the key elements of edible garden design—basically, you need to work out what you want to grow, what your site conditions are, what will best suit your lifestyle, and what design you want.

MENU

Growing edibles is easy and rewarding. First you need to decide what you want to eat, then you simply plant. Let your menu be the driver, your masterplan. You can then work out how best to grow those foods in your conditions.

It's all about what you love to eat. Be realistic about which edible plants you and your family will actually eat and how you want to eat them. Growing your own food is a golden opportunity to learn about nutrition and well-being, so don't just consider the flavors you love but the vitamins you need as well (see the table on the facing page). Think of the peace of mind you will have knowing that your food will be free of toxic pesticides and is not genetically modified. This is very important to me and my family, as I'm sure it is to you; we need to preserve our heirloom varieties.

One of the best ways to begin thinking about what you want to grow is to attach a yearly schedule to the fridge, showing your favorite plants grouped by climate zone and season: when to sow, when to harvest, and when to let seed. Create a personalized list of seasonal foods, and you will be harvesting the fruits of your own labor for the family table in no time.

We're free to eat whatever we want even without a garden. Consider growing more unusual types of fruits and vegetables, such as heirloom varieties that grow well and taste great. Heirloom plants are open-pollinated cultivars, and were common in the past, but over the years have been discarded for more commercially viable varieties. Unlike modern hybrids, heirlooms have great flavor and some have natural resistance to pests and disease. They have not been genetically engineered either.

THE DELICIOUS DESIGN PHILOSOPHY

Kids and edibles

In my experience, kids tend to write the rules on the fruit and vegetables they will eat. Busy parents can very easily fall into the trap of giving them only the basics or their favorites.

One big bonus about growing your own edibles is that, if you get the kids involved, there is a pretty good chance that they will expand their fruit and veggie repertoire. They will love the fact that Brussels sprouts grow off the stem of the plant, or that peanuts come out of the ground, just like potatoes and carrots. As they start to become more excited about where their food comes from, and the fact that it seems to be growing out of thin air, kids will naturally become more adventurous about trying new foods.

Let's face it—it's far more exciting to pull a carrot out of the ground than a biscuit from the tin!

IF YOU VISIT MY WEBSITE, JAMIEDURIE.COM YOU CAN DOWNLOAD FOR FREE A SEASONAL PLANT SOW & HARVEST CHART AS WELL AS A SEASONAL DESIGN FEATURES AND PLANTING TIPS CHART.

FUNCTIONAL ANALYSIS

There are a number of things to consider when you are conducting your functional analysis—here are the main ones.

The basics
Draw an outline of the space and indicate:
- access points
- north, south, east, and west
- gradient or slope
- prevailing winds—is the site windy or sheltered?

Water
- Do you have water access?
- How much natural rainfall do you receive?
- Can you integrate a water tank into your space?
- Will you need irrigation?

Soil
- Is it a sandy soil?
- Is it a clay soil?
- Does it drain well?
- Are there depth restrictions?
- What's the soil's pH level (acidic or alkaline)?

Light
- Which areas are shady and which are sunny?
- Are there any views to retain or block?
- Are there any trees in the garden?
- Will the canopy of any trees shade the garden?

CONDITIONS

Planning your edible garden

Good garden design is all about addressing not just your needs but also your plants' needs, and understanding your site's constraints and opportunities. Ultimately, your aim is to create a space that is functional and attractive, with a mixture of carefully selected plants strategically placed where they will best thrive—a place where people want to spend time.

Planning ahead is essential. You might want to work it out for yourself, or get a professional involved at this stage. Either way, you need to spend some time in and around your garden, getting to know the conditions, before you start. There are a number of questions worth asking yourself—it's called conducting a functional analysis.

- How do you currently use the garden?
- How would you like to use your garden in the future?
- What activities do you and your family imagine taking place within it?
- How will the new plan affect the family pets?

Take a sheet of paper, draw the boundaries of your garden, and then mark where the house is. On a new piece of paper, write a list of all the ways you want to use your garden. It might include: reading the weekend papers in a sun-drenched lounge area; lunching with the family in an outdoor dining area with a barbecue; taking an afternoon nap in a nice shady spot; soaking in a spa (in privacy); catching a movie or a bit of sport on the TV outdoors with the family; or gathering round the eco-fireplace with friends in comfy armchairs for a cup of coffee and a chat. You get the idea.

Now, simply watch where the sun falls on your garden and mark bubbles on the plan showing where you want your activities to take place—where you want to position the furniture, the barbecue, the spa, the kids' area, and the fireplace. If, for example, you only really use the garden in the afternoon, you would note where the sun falls in the backyard in the afternoon and place your chaise lounge there. If you have only one spot for your outdoor dining table and you see that it gets sun all day, you know you will need to use an umbrella, build a pergola, or plant the right edible shade tree. Make sure you also take into account the shadowlines of the house and curious neighbors peeping into your backyard.

You have now designed a garden to suit your needs—the only thing left is to plug in the edible plants. Bear in mind that most edibles need at least four hours of direct sunlight a day (see page 32), so they should be planted in the parts of your garden that get reliable sun.

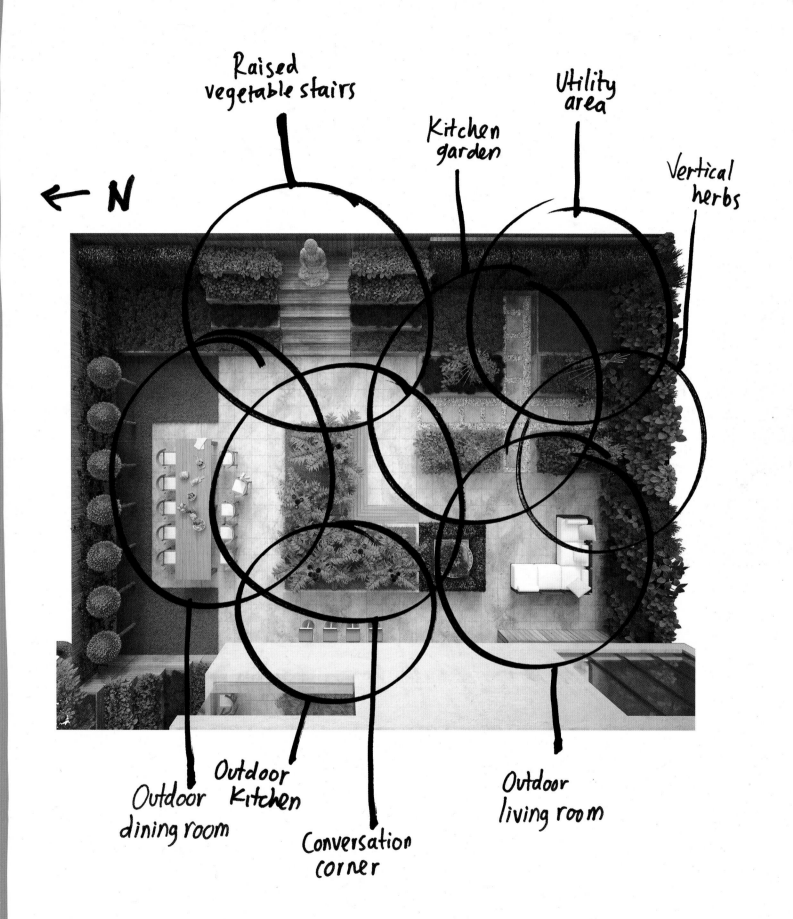

Raised
vegetable stairs

Kitchen
garden

Utility
area

Vertical
herbs

← N

Outdoor
dining room

Outdoor
Kitchen

Conversation
corner

Outdoor
living room

This outdoor bath has made
my Sydney garden my sanctuary.
Placement is paramount,
and my outdoor bathtub was
no exception. It gets good sun,
the surrounding foliage creates
privacy, and I have food at
my fingertips.

A microclimate

Some edibles can be taken out of their comfort zone by using innovative garden structures and clever thinking to create a microclimate that is right for them. If you learn how to control the environment like this, you will expand your available choices of edible plants.

Throughout my travels over the years, I have discovered all manner of interesting herbs, vegetables, fruits, and spices growing in extreme conditions in extraordinary places—locations where some people would say it's impossible to grow anything. One example is the incredible Himalayan greenhouses on pages 54-57, which are under snow for most of the year. Extreme temperatures will destroy a plant's cellular structure, causing sunburn (in hot climates) or frost damage (in freezing climates), and once a plant has had cellular damage there's no turning back—the damage has to be pruned out to allow any hope of regrowth. Greenhouses can help prevent that damage occurring. Technology and innovation have allowed people to leap over horticultural hurdles in a single bound. If you're willing to create the right microclimate, amazing things are possible.

Even within your own backyard there'll be a number of different microclimates under trees or in small valleys, so don't underestimate how far you can push the seasons or the plant species. Play with the topography of the land; creating microclimates in dips and valleys and planting canopy trees are some easy ways to control the environment.

To create a true microclimate, look at what makes your chosen edibles suffer or thrive. Then, all you need to do is provide protection from what makes the plant suffer, and serve up the elements that make it thrive.

Heat and wind can increase transpiration, causing plants to lose both moisture and nutrients. You can plant large canopy plants to protect your edibles from harsh sun, although do make sure a little dappled sun can get through. A canopy will also protect the more delicate plants from frost, which can be incredibly harmful to plants. To protect your edibles from prevailing winds, you can plant dense shrubs or thick hedges around them.

You'll be wasting money unless the microclimate in your garden suits your edibles. The best way to get the information that you need is to do your research and speak to your local nursery or a local expert—you will save yourself a lot of time and money in the long run.

This shade structure creates an ideal microclimate for the plants it houses.

LIFESTYLE

Before you sit down to design your edible garden, there is one more thing you need to consider—your lifestyle. What is the design that will fit in best with your lifestyle? You should factor in the following:

Your budget

It is important to have a clear understanding of your project budget before you start, since that will determine what materials and plants you can afford and, therefore, the look and feel of your garden.

Your budget is also relevant at the next stage. Once you have your garden design, it's up to you to carry out the plan according to your budget. Be realistic about what's possible. If you are planning to design something on a grand scale, always consider seeking advice from an expert—high-end design comes at a price. Remember that you can have a wonderful edible garden without spending a fortune—growing food requires just plants (or seeds), sunlight, water, and time. If you can afford to do it all at once, then go for it. But if you need to roll out the plan over a longer period of time, I suggest you start your growing investment with the more permanent bones of the garden, as they will take a while to establish.

Your time

Do you have any time restraints? More to the point, what time do you have?

Be realistic about what time you have available. Set yourself an achievable goal, such as spending ten minutes a day nurturing your plants. It's different for everyone—whether you are at home most of the day or at work most of the day, it's all about designing a garden and choosing the plants to suit your lifestyle. It might help if you think of time spent in the garden as free therapy!

Your space

Edibles can be integrated into any space, no matter how big or small. We come in all shapes and sizes and so do plants, so make sure you choose the right companions for you! Be practical about your choice of garden design and always run large plans or additions by your local government agency. If it's your first edible garden, it's a good idea to start small—as your gardening knowledge and confidence grow, so will the scope of your garden. Here are a few ideas for different spaces.

Family spaces

You will have covered this already when you completed your functional analysis, but I wanted to give you a friendly reminder. If you have the space, try to create zones and outdoor rooms so everyone can enjoy the garden in different ways. Consider creating a safe, child-friendly nook that's hidden away, so kids can claim a space as their own and the grown-ups don't have to contend with the mess. This will provide kids with independence, creative freedom, and memories of playing in the garden that will last a lifetime. Of course, it's also important to create areas for adult retreat and downtime!

Rented spaces

Ease of mobility and portable structures are vital when you move around a lot. You can put castors or wheels onto just about any garden structure or opt for small pots or vertical walls to give you maximum flexibility. Growing plants in portable structures allows you to shift their location to catch the sun, and also makes it easy when you move. The veggie gardens at my own home are quick to install and without fixed bases, so they can be easily transported—they are like giant egg rings!

Shared spaces

University students are not the only ones who share their spaces. Communal, multi-generational living is a fact of life these days and it's important to consider how to share a garden as well as a fridge. As with many things, communication is key, and using a few labels to stake your claim comes in handy, too. Gardening together is a fun, healthy way to connect with the people you live with. You'll actually find that it becomes a whole new way to socialize—I call it the "garden glue."

Community spaces

Whether you live in an urban, suburban, or rural area, community gardens are a destination for people of like minds to come together. Community spaces are popping up all over the country, and around the globe. They are a great way for people with no available space to get together and share the rewards that an edible garden can bring. Many hands, and minds, make light work. You can join an existing community garden or enlist some friends and start one yourself.

DESIGN

Now for the fun bit. Once you have done your homework and figured out what works for you, your conditions, and your lifestyle, you're free to design to your heart's content.

Start with a design plan—you can do it yourself, or work with a professional. Either way, ask yourself the following questions:

- Are there any personal elements or design features that you would like to include in the design?
- Is there a particular style of garden you like or dislike?
- What materials, designs, and colors have you used in your house? How can you bring them out into the garden?

Look through magazines and browse the Internet for inspiration. And remember—there's no reason why a productive garden can't be as beautiful as an ornamental one. As I mentioned, I even have an outdoor bath next to my veggie patch in the front garden (see the photo on pages 18–19). Once you plant for privacy, anything is possible!

I like to design with color and shapes in mind. You also need to consider height, future growth, and seasonal constraints, as what's colorful now may not be next season.

Designing with color

When it comes to edibles, composing a living color palette can be slightly tricky, but also quite fun. Some of the most beautiful and unexpected colors come from everyday fruits and vegetables—and even herbs. It's just that we don't usually consider edibles from a design perspective.

When you focus purely on color, your palette will start to jump out at you. You'll notice the red stems on rhubarb; the bright yellows and magentas in spinach leaves; kale is an obvious showstopper; while rosemary and oregano provide a stable, muted backdrop. There's nothing as vivid, in terms of green, as a dense mass of parsley. The fruit of cumquats, mandarins, lemons, and oranges are long lasting and durable, while the silver serrated leaves of the artichoke and the architectural stature of a pineapple make great accents.

I'M HOPING BY NOW YOU ARE STARTING
TO CREATE A VISION FOR YOUR OWN EDIBLE GARDEN DESIGN.
HAVE A LOOK AT THE COLOUR WHEEL WE'VE CREATED BELOW,
FILLED WITH EDIBLES, TO GET YOU STARTED.

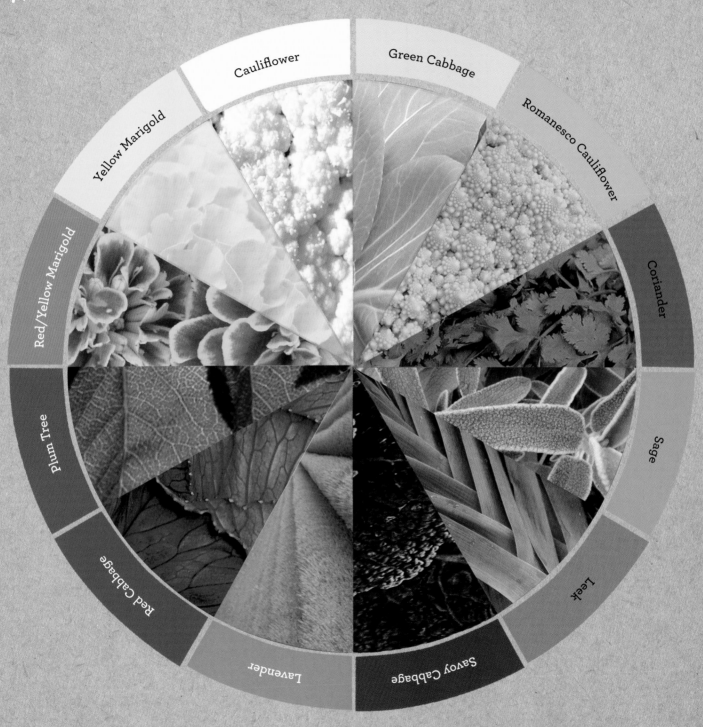

Designing with shapes first and plants later

There are so many clever ways to integrate edibles into your existing landscape. I like to start by designing with shapes to create a functional and design-focused space, with different focal points, as I have done with the citrus canopy on page 10.

We all know how it feels to be in a comfortable living room. Simply imagine replacing the walls, ceilings, and floors with plants. By using plants to construct the space, you're creating a living, breathing environment—living architecture. Just make sure that you factor in how the plant will change as it matures (for example, the ultimate spread and height of a tree or the ferocity of a climbing plant), do your research, and never hesitate to ask an expert. Here are some edible plant shapes to consider.

CEILINGS AND CANOPIES

Round canopy
citrus, pomegranate, apple, avocado, peach

Vase canopy
pomegranate, lychee

Weeping canopy
mulberry

Conical canopy
pear, bay

Umbrella canopy
citrus, walnut, avocado, peach, lychee

Ball canopy
walnut, fig

Lateral canopy
fig

WALLS

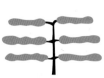

Scrambling climber
cucumber, sweet pea

Twining climber
kiwifruit, bean

Tendril climber
passion fruit

Espalier
fruit trees, such as pear, apple, and peach, can be shaped into espalier style

BORDERS

Clump arching
rhubarb, eggplant, swiss chard, chard

Clump spreading
garlic, onion

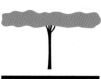

Clump forming shrub
blueberry, rosemary, lavender, sage, dill

FLOORS

Tufting upright
strawberry, parsley

Spreading ground cover
mint, oregano

Matting ground cover
thyme, marjoram

ACCENTS

Fan
artichoke

Lollipop canopy
Herbs and fruits such as bay, lemon, orange, and lime can be clipped into a "standard" or "lollipop" shape

Integration

You can be creative in how you integrate your edible plants into your garden design. What you want is a garden that gives you pleasure while you are creating and maintaining it, and is also a space to enjoy, filled with thriving plants to nourish you.

Not everyone has the budget or space to create their ideal edible landscape. Like most endeavours, it's about compromise or creativity, or a mixture of both.

Some suggestions

If you want a kitchen garden, why not do something a bit modern and incorporate edible plants into the garden as a whole, creating an edible landscape. That's the whole purpose of this book! Edible plants don't need to be segregated. Most fruiting plants and herbs love the sun, so choose their locations carefully to provide sun for at least a few hours every day, even in winter.

Instead of growing a standard box hedge, use rosemary (for its scent and to flavor roast lamb) or sage. Use ground covers such as mint or thyme at the edge of steppers or paths to fill gaps and soften boundaries.

Some of the best small trees for suburban gardens are fruiting trees—think orange, lemon, lime, cumquat, and olive. Bay trees have lovely fragrant leaves that are great to flavor casseroles and other meals. Deciduous fruit trees such as cherry, plum, and apple let the sun in during winter, blossom beautifully in spring, and offer fruit in summer. There are many new dwarf varieties of fruit trees available from nurseries. You can also get a range of plum, nectarine, peach, and apple dwarf cultivars to grow in small spaces such as courtyards, balconies, or even in pots.

Consider climbers, too. Plant passion fruit or kiwifruit to screen a fence. Some veggies grow very well in pots, including cucumber, eggplant, and spinach. If space is tight, consider varieties of tomatoes and climbing beans that can be trained to grow up trellises. And if you have only the tiniest garden, fill a north-facing window box with a selection of your favorite herbs.

Explore the wonderful variety of foliage color and texture with the range of cultivars now available; vibrant chilli, ornamental lettuce, and chocolate-scented mint can also add a bit of fun.

Access

Think about how you will get to your edibles. The key is to make sure the height is right, so you don't have to bend down too low or reach up too high when maintaining and picking. You might choose a raised bed, a combination of pots, or a vertical wall planted out with assorted herbs and some "go to" ingredients. Also consider placing a planter box behind a seated area, so you can catch the scent of herbs floating by.

Imagine being able to pick a sprig of coriander, mint, or Thai basil and throw it into your stir-fry on the barbecue wok. Or picking a lime or lemon from your tree to garnish a cold drink. When you grow your own produce, you'll know it's free from toxic chemicals, and you can share your bounty with family and friends with confidence. Your children will love growing cherry tomatoes, strawberries, and mushrooms—and they are much more likely to eat them if they have helped harvest them.

At various points in each chapter I will be giving you specific advice on certain issues. I am calling these sections "Down and dirty," because this is where you'll be really getting stuck into it!

WATER

Generally speaking, edible gardens, like ornamental gardens, need reliable water. Many edibles are seasonal, so they need plenty of water and nutrients during their growing season to ensure good food production.

Of course, a rainwater tank is essential. Not only is it a great way to make use of a free, natural resource, but it will cut down your water bills, too! There is a range of options available—from large underground storage units and slim-line tanks that fit between your house and side boundary to simple, homemade water vessels such as a secondhand oak wine barrel or an old bath.

Hand-watering tips

Many of us water by hand as it's cost effective and relatively easy. The downside is that it's difficult to ensure all the plants get equal water distribution—and sometimes we simply forget to do it! But if you have a small space and a good memory, hand watering is a great way of keeping tabs on the goings-on in your garden.

Bear in mind:

- It's best to water your garden deeply and less frequently. Aim for approximately two minutes of watering per square yard.

- As a general rule, water your garden every second day in summer, and around twice a week in winter.

- Group plants with similar water requirements together. Perennial edibles such as rosemary, sage, thyme, and oregano will require less water than fast-growing annuals such as tomatoes, cucumber, and basil.

- Use a thick blanket of organic mulch, such as hay or straw, to reduce evaporation from your soil and help keep the plants' roots moist for longer.

- Keep up-to-date with watering restrictions for your local area.

Automated irrigation

If you want to set up a drip irrigation system, speak to an expert about application rates, water distribution, and system maintenance. The crops you are growing, your soil type, and the time of year will determine your application rates and spacing of drippers. In my opinion, a drip irrigation system is the most efficient and targeted form of irrigation, as it has a very low evaporation rate compared to sprinkling systems.

LIGHT

This refers to the amount of sunlight your plant needs to thrive—it is the "photo" part of photosynthesis.

The ideal conditions for edibles are:

- full sun
- north-facing
- protected from wind
- protected from frost

Some edible plants can manage with the available light, but others can't tolerate too much or too little sun, so do your research. Be clever with making your conditions work for your plants. For example, position your edibles in a north-facing aspect to make the most of the sun's natural path.

Here are some examples of the light requirements of some common edibles:

- **<u>Full sun (six to eight hours of direct sunlight each day):</u>** Edibles from warm climates or drought-tolerant areas, such as citrus fruit trees, rosemary, sage, tomatoes, basil, and pumpkin do well in these conditions.

- **<u>Part sun and part shade (four to six hours of direct sunlight each day):</u>** Most edibles (and plants in general) thrive in these conditions. Partial shade conditions may be created by nearby buildings, structures, or trees. Factor in these details when you do your site assessment. You could grow slightly more hardy plants like lettuce, Asian greens, spinach, leeks, radish, or watercress.

It is difficult to grow edibles in areas that get less than four hours of sunlight a day, although you might have some success with sprouts, mung beans, and alfalfa. You could also consider creating your own microclimate by building a greenhouse or planting protector plants, with dense foliage, around the outside or over the top of the edibles.

SOIL AND NUTRIENTS

Soil structure is the key to a thriving garden, because soil is the source of nutrients, minerals, micro-organisms, and support for your plants.

In particular, topsoil is a hugely valuable commodity and maintaining it is crucial. Soil preparation—such as cultivating deeply or adding organic matter—will help to establish plants and encourage them to thrive. Well-prepared topsoil fosters better water penetration (which prevents run off and erosion), improves root penetration, and aerates the soil.

If you have the space and can invest your time, begin composting or start a worm farm—the nutrient-rich "liquid gold" that's produced is priceless. It helps achieve the optimum pH levels for nutrient production, which in turn feeds the plants.

Well-drained soil on a level surface, preferably raised, is best; however, not everyone has these ideal conditions. To help you along the way, we have included soil preparation advice throughout this book.

Soil

Whether your soil is sandy or clay, it will benefit from the addition of organic matter, which adds structure to sandy soils and helps to manage soils with too much clay. The result is an easy-to-dig loamy soil that retains moisture well. With any soil, it is important to add organic matter or compost to improve it after harvesting or each season.

Soil additives

There are many soil additives that can be used to improve soil, depending upon what the problem is. Here are some of the most common:

- **gypsum:** controls pH level of the soil and also breaks up clay.
- **lime:** controls pH level of the soil and also breaks up clay.
- **blood and bone:** adds high amounts of nitrogen for an instant boost of nutrients that improve leaf growth.
- **seaweed extracts:** adds high amounts of nitrogen for an instant boost of nutrients that improve leaf growth.
- **manure:** helps improve soil quality, by providing nutrients, better drainage, and better moisture retention.
- **mushroom compost:** helps improve soil quality, by providing nutrients, better drainage, and better moisture retention.
- **worm castings:** an extremely high source of organic nutrients, best used when diluted in water to create "worm tea."
- **peat moss:** provides soil nutrients and generally enhances soil quality by improving moisture retention and drainage.

TOOLS OF THE TRADE

Here is a list of my can't-do-without edible garden tools. See my website for the printable version. There are great agrarian tools to suit all budgets and styles at nurseries and hardware stores. You can also find some wonderful pre-loved tools at markets, garage sales, and secondhand stores.

Store your tools somewhere that is accessible, but also child safe. If you have the luxury of a shed, you are one of the lucky ones, but if your space is limited don't despair; create a vertical storage system with shelving or hooks or, even better, use a portable workman's belt or tool box that can be stored indoors.

Do love your tools! If you look after them, they are a great investment. Always clean them after each use by washing with water and drying with a cloth.

Soil

Plants

Pots

Seeds

Trowel

Hand fork

Watering can

Bucket (great for mixing and/ or moving small loads from A to B)

Water spray (great for indoor plants)

Pruning shears

Scissors for pruning

Hose with trigger

Labels (optional)

Colander (to collect your harvest)

Preparation tray or area

Compost bucket

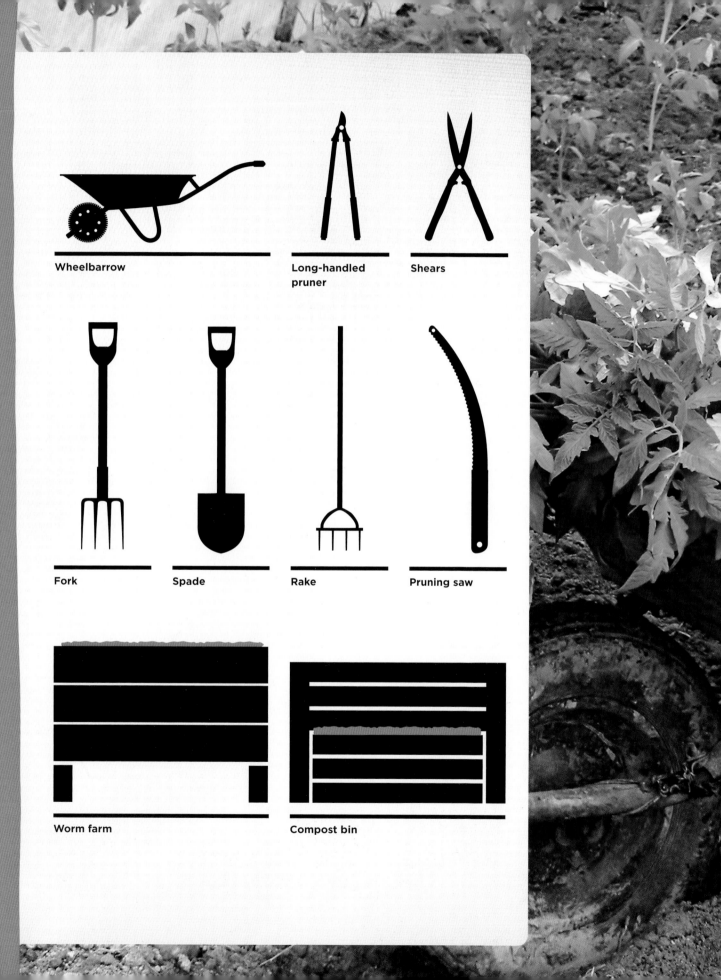

Wheelbarrow

Long-handled pruner

Shears

Fork

Spade

Rake

Pruning saw

Worm farm

Compost bin

1. Garden steps

Maximize a slope or different levels in a garden by creating garden steps. To gain maximum depth, you can design a garden step in reverse—with planting beds that are deeper than they are wide. It's a fantastic way to grow edibles, and the steps can be as short or long as you like, depending on your space.

Remember that all gardens need reliable drainage so they don't develop fungal diseases or anaerobic soils. When you plant on a slope, you're guaranteed that a garden step will retain the precious topsoil, while the sub-layer allows the water to drain away.

Have a look later in this chapter at how I have used garden steps in my garden in Los Angeles (see pages 42-49).

2. Vertical pockets

Vertical pockets are a great way to make the most of vertical surfaces without sacrificing valuable green space. There are some fantastic options available or you could create your own version.

After creating many inner-city vertical gardens over the years, my team and I designed a greenwall blanket that is super easy to install and can be made in a size to fit your fence, balcony, or wall. Plants grow in the pockets, just like they would in a pot—it gives you a wonderfully "full" look, rather than just seeing vertical strips of plants. You can plant directly into the wide, deep pockets, which are attached to a waterproof backing that is then connected to a secure structure. Some versions, including mine, have an internal drip irrigation system, and this is what I would always recommend. Consult a professional before attaching them to an existing wall or structure—check out my website to learn more.

I used vertical pockets when I installed the vertical garden at Cromer Community Center (see page 108).

3. Greenwall A-frames

This variation of the vertical wall or vertical pocket is ideal if you rent, or if you don't have walls or a structure to support a vertical garden. The A-frame structure could even be mounted on castors (wheels) so you can move it around to follow the sun or move house easily. Remember, the more vertical surface area, the more food you can grow.

Have a look at the A-frames I used in the Los Angeles garden of Seth and Samantha Barnes (see pages 100-107).

4

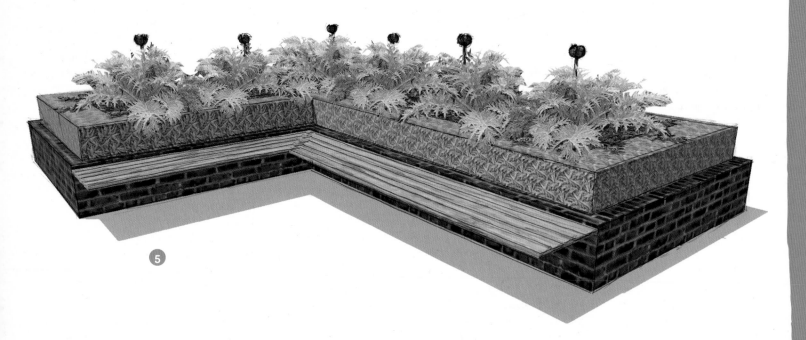

5

4. Teepee climber frames

This traditional design looks great and it's very functional. It not only adds height and architecture to your overall garden design, but it's also easy to reach without having to bend down. It's a cubist vertical trellis that allows the peas or beans to climb upward and even to choose their favorite side. If you like this shape and have problems with pests, birds, or vermin, a similar yet larger teepee-shaped netted canopy will protect edibles planted beneath. This structure is easy to assemble and can fit into a variety of spaces, while still allowing for more vertical climbing structures or vertical habit edibles.

I used teepee-shaped netted canopies in the edible garden of Irena and Jeremy Hutchings at Paperbark Camp, Jervis Bay (see pages 132-133).

5. Raised beds

Making a raised garden for your edibles is easy, and it allows you to get to your plants without bending over, provides seating on the surrounding bed walls, and gives the plants the depth and drainage they require to thrive. A good height guide is somewhere between 14 and 23 inches high, and if you want a seat I'd suggest between 10 and 23 inches max. When you are planning the size of your raised bed, always make sure you can easily reach into its center without having to crawl over any plants. Some small steppers may be all you need. My clever mum, Joy Durie (see her story on pages 124-131) has placed small walking planks to help her navigate her way around her raised garden beds.

Remember, if you are creating raised beds, you'll be changing the level of the garden (which I often do anyway from a design perspective to create interest and intrigue). You will need to secure the wood or railroad ties around the outside, using a string line and level. Get the level up nice and high and, if necessary, secure the corners with a corner bracket. Make sure you fill the bed with good soil, mix in organic matter, and organic fertilizer and your plants will thrive. Then plant away, remembering to till or turn the soil in between harvests.

Put a wheel on it! I love these planter boxes on castors—they add so much versatility, and can be moved in and out of the sun as desired. Imagine them around a dining setting . . . true delicious design.

There wouldn't be much point in me banging on about the virtues of edible gardening if I hadn't embraced it myself. So, let me tell you about the edible garden I have created for my home in Los Angeles. I planted my entire edible patch on a forty-five-degree slope of loose, decomposed granite, which was high in nutrients but highly susceptible to erosion. I combated that by installing a series of terraces to stop the erosion and to preserve the nutrients, moisture, and soil structure, so that the edibles could thrive. This is a valuable tool for anyone with a sloping block.

ABOUT THE GARDEN

In my Los Angeles garden there are no fences, just walls embedded with vertical lush greenery. This is one of the great benefits of a vertical garden—goodbye fence and hello garden. A major feature is my gabion bowls, which are positioned throughout the garden, to add a dramatic extension to my planting area. They are giant bowl-shaped cages filled with loose stones that hold the soil in place and provide excellent drainage. These are my signature planters that I have used in private gardens and resorts all over the world.

The ultimate chill-out zone is the poolside lounge. I wanted the area to feel lush and enclosed, so I covered the walls with vertical garden pockets. Textural, edible plants such as sage, nasturtiums, and strawberries spill down from the walls, providing a sense of shelter. Pushing the garden up the wall also allowed me maximum space around the pool.

It was challenging being both client and designer. Because I have spent so many years designing other people's gardens, traveling and being inspired by amazing gardens around the world, I was anything but short of ideas! One of my primary inspirations was renowned Sri Lankan architect and landscape designer Geoffrey Bawa. He sculpted landscapes for people to enjoy—he really was the master, a true pioneer of extending the home into the garden.

Sustainability and respect for the environment are always at the forefront of my mind in my approach to design projects, so for my own home, here are some of the environmentally friendly features I incorporated:

- recycled paving stones
- composite decking made up of 97 percent recycled materials
- a vertical wall garden made of geotextile fabric from recycled plastic bottles
- the roof garden over the outdoor dining room, with its 6-inch sustainable "green" roof, controling the transfer of heat into the dwellings below and reducing energy costs
- the mulch in the garden, made from recycled demolition lumber
- the pool is heated by solar energy and uses a zero-chemical UV ozone filter whose ultraviolet light kills pathogens and bacteria
- the irrigation system is a computer-controlled, drip irrigation system to minimize water use and evaporation
- the entire paved backyard drains into the pool, harvesting any excess rainwater into the balance tank of the pool.

I like to plant edibles where they can be used to their maximum potential. In my L.A. garden I designed garden steps and vertical walls for easy access near the outdoor kitchen and dining areas.

The thing that gives me so much joy with this garden is that here you can do every single thing you do indoors, only you're outside—cooking, eating, sleeping, even bathing! I especially love cooking for friends in my outdoor kitchen, positioned between the outdoor dining area and my vegetable garden. There is nothing better than being able to pick fresh produce and moments later add it to your meal! I designed stepped garden beds for just this purpose, to allow more plants to be grown in a smaller space on a steep slope that leads to my design studio.

I think it's important for every garden to have a sense of luxury, and my own garden is no exception. I designed a series of cushioned oversized lounges that line the narrow space between the reclad swimming pool and the old perimeter fence—now a vertical garden. A cozy sunken sitting area and fire pit have also been added to the mix, making outdoor entertaining possible at any time of year.

BEST FEATURES

I love absolutely everything about this garden, but here are some of the highlights:

- **Zoning:** There are various functional outdoor rooms within the garden that can be used for different purposes. This encourages us to spend more time outdoors—cooking, relaxing, or swimming, and as the sun moves so can we.

- **Use of space:** Every available square inch of space has been used to create an inviting, interesting, urban sanctuary, with a very productive garden. I like to be surrounded by as much greenery as possible, and vertical gardens help me achieve this—I also benefit from the lateral space that the vertical garden allows.

- **Connecting indoors and out:** I am passionate about blurring the boundaries between inside and outside. In my garden, I have taken this to the extreme! I actually knocked out one wall of my bedroom and replaced it with twin pivoting panels covered in orchids and tropical plants—each panel opens to the garden, flooding the room with breezes, scents, and sounds every morning; it's amazing to wake up to!

YOU COULD DO THIS

The principles I used to design my Los Angeles garden can be translated to any space, anywhere. It's all about drawing the indoors outside—I simply turned every room inside out and mirrored it outside. How you do this depends upon your location, garden size, and climate. Draw inspiration from your surroundings and ask yourself the following questions:

- What architectural style is your home?
- What plants grow well in your local area?
- How cold does it get in winter, how hot in summer?
- What are your favorite activities and how can you take them outdoors?

The answers to these questions will start you on the pathway to creating your very own garden sanctuary.

IN MY LOS ANGELES GARDEN
I GROW FORTY-FIVE EDIBLES,
INCLUDING:

APPLES

ASPARAGUS

BASIL

BAY TREES

BLACKBERRIES

BLUEBERRIES

CHAMOMILE

CHILLIES

CHIVES

CHOCOLATE MINT

COMMON MINT

FIGS

GRAPES

KIWIFRUIT

LIMES

PASSION FRUIT

PEACHES

PUMPKINS

RASPBERRIES

ROSEMARY

SAGE

SHALLOTS

SPEARMINT

TOMATOES

CHAPTER TWO

EDIBLES ANYWHERE

You can grow edible plants in containers anywhere you choose. They are literally a moveable feast. You don't need to sacrifice green space or living space—just be creative about how you use it. From New York City to the harsh mountaintops of the Himalayas, there is always a solution.

WHAT'S IT ALL ABOUT?

—— You can incorporate edibles into your life wherever you live. For many people, the easiest way to do this is to grow them indoors — they look great perched on window-sills and tucked into sunny corners. But don't let your imagination stop there. I have been totally inspired by my travels to think of new and creative ways to grow edibles in a limited space.

In Europe, even the smallest courtyards and windowsills look so inviting, with plants squeezed into every nook and cranny; Japan and China lead the world in green, edible rooftops, while in the developing world people make great use of recycled and raw materials. It's all about resourcefulness — understanding your conditions and working with what you have.

So, let's get started — the sky's the limit (literally, the highest rooftop garden I know of is in the Himalayas). If you have a courtyard or balcony, install some containers filled with edibles. If you don't, try window boxes. Have you thought about planting on your roof? What about verge gardening (local government permitting)? If your garden is big enough, you might even consider a greenhouse. Just grab a container and start planting.

LILLE FRO GREENHOUSE PROGRAM, HIMALAYAS

Ladakh in the Himalayas in northern India is one of the driest places in the world. The growing season is only four months long, so there's a lack of food in winter, causing villagers to suffer from poor nutrition and other health problems. Lille Fro aims to improve farming practices so the villagers can have fresh fruit and veggies year-round. It does this by teaching the local community how to build and maintain greenhouses.

The greenhouses are made from locally produced mud bricks and lined with straw, so that heat from the sun is retained at night, when it's needed most. One side of the roof is covered with transparent polythene sheeting (more durable and cheaper than glass), which allows radiation to pass through and minimizes heat loss. I really like the simple, smart design and, apart from raising awareness of their amazing work, that's one of the reasons I wanted to feature Lille Fro in this book. This design can easily be translated into anyone's garden and you could build it using a variety of materials.

Thanks to the greenhouses, the local people now have a year-round supply of fresh fruit and vegetables, including tomatoes and zucchini in summer and spinach, coriander, and carrots in winter. They even generate income by selling the surplus. How good is that?

WHO OR WHAT INSPIRES ME?

LILLE FRO IS DANISH FOR LITTLE FROG AND ALSO MEANS NEW BEGINNINGS, IN THE FORM OF A LITTLE SEED.

THERE IS AN EXPRESSION IN DANISH:

IF YOU PLANT A LITTLE SEED, SPRINKLE IT WITH LOVE, TALK TO IT AND SHOW THAT YOU CARE, LET IT KNOW YOU ARE THERE, UNDOUBTEDLY, A BEAUTIFUL TREE WILL GROW.

The Lille Fro Greenhouse Program is an inspiration to people living in harsh conditions all over the world.

Who or what inspires m

Groups of women manage the day-to-day running of the greenhouses, which provide the community with fresh fruit and vegetables all year round.

ROPPONGI NOUEN FARM, TOKYO

Trust the Japanese to come up with a solution that is as stunning as it is practical. Right in the center of Tokyo, in one of the main nightlife districts, you'll find Roppongi Nouen Farm, a greenhouse made up of eight stacked glass cubes, whose produce is used by the restaurant next door. The gardens are managed by farming families, who lease the containers and cultivate the plants. Now that's what I call innovative. It often frustrates me that greenhouses are used purely for their horticultural function, but these guys have created something like architectural installation art, and I love it.

THE SPOTTED PIG, NEW YORK CITY

Every time I visit New York, I eat at least one meal at The Spotted Pig in Greenwich Village. It is an absolute cracker of a place, and my favorite spot for brunch with friends. Chef April Bloomfield has created a neighborhood institution with her much-loved British pub food with a Manhattan twist. The Spotted Pig was one of the first gastropubs in New York—now they are springing up everywhere.

The restaurant is also a great example of how to grow edibles indoors—they have totally integrated the plants into the lived-in look and feel of the space. The wide-ledged windowsills are crammed with recycled tins planted out with a variety of flowers and herbs, which are used in everything from the garnishes to the drinks. The plants are also used to create "walls" or intimate spaces within the restaurant and to give the whole place a sense of privacy; diners feel hidden away as they watch the world go by outside. The footpath outside the restaurant is also packed with a great collection of planted containers. And their famous burger with shoestring fries is unbelievable.

DOWN AND DIRTY

CONTAINER GARDENING

The best advice I can give you if you plan to start some container gardening is to choose containers that are nonpermeable, so that the nutrients, water, oxygen and trace elements all land where they are needed most—in the root system. Terracotta, clay and other unsealed pots tend to draw out both the moisture and nutrients, placing the plant under a lot of stress. I often use Perspex to grow my edibles, because it is completely nonpermeable and doesn't allow any of the moisture or nutrients to escape. I also believe that when the plant's roots hit the slippery surface they continue to grow around it, whereas rough surfaces can stunt their growth. Plus, if you use clear Perspex containers you get to see right through to the plant's roots and the dirt that it's growing in—pretty cool!

Edible plants grown in containers need a rich potting mix with sufficient nutrients and good water-holding capacity. It's best not to use soil in pots, as it can be very heavy when wet and poor drainage can be a problem. Potting mix dries out more quickly than soil though, so keep an eye on the moisture levels of your edibles and research their water needs so you don't overwater or underwater. Mulching will help with water retention, and can also supply nutrients to the plant.

Tips and tricks

Here are a few handy tips that will help keep your container edibles thriving:

- Rotate the container 180 degrees every few weeks to even out the light source. This is easier if you have castors on the base of large containers.
- Don't be afraid to replant every few years. I don't think plants should sit in containers for any longer than two years, as they start to get a bit tired and starved of nutrients.
- To give your plants a nutrient boost, use a quick-acting liquid fertilizer for fast-growing annuals such as tomatoes, spinach, and basil, or a slow-release fertilizer for perennials like rosemary, thyme, and oregano.
- Use wetting agents to help the root system retain moisture.
- Make sure the plants have proper drainage. If necessary, drill holes in the bottom of the container.
- Research the origin of your plants to find out how much water and sunlight they need. Rosemary, for example, is a Mediterranean plant that is in the sun all day, so it needs as much light as you can give it.

There are endless possibilities with container gardening. I planted these low, clear acrylic troughs with an edible hedge that changes from rosemary to parsley and then basil, and runs the whole length of my Sydney balcony.

INDOOR CONTAINER EDIBLES

If you live in an urban area, chances are you won't have a backyard or even a balcony. The solution is to grow plants such as herbs, edible flowers, and sprouts indoors. Think about your plant menu, then assess your indoor conditions.

Menu—which edibles can you grow indoors?

I incorporate edible plants into my everyday life as much as I can—to eat and as design accents. I also love the element of wellness that they bring into my home.

Be practical about your choice of indoor edibles. Ask yourself, "What edible plants will I use regularly?" Here are some suggestions:

- **Eating:** Try growing basil, chervil, chives, parsley, lettuce, mint, nasturtium, tarragon, thyme, and Vietnamese mint.
- **Drinking:** Consider the teas you like and flavors that you can add to juices and cocktails. Choose from apple mint, chamomile, chocolate mint, lemon verbena, mint, peppermint, pineapple mint, spearmint, and tea jasmine.
- **Bathing:** Enrich your bathing space with edible, fragrant, or medicinal plants, such as aloe vera, basil, chamomile, lemon balm, mint, and sweet violet.
- **Design:** Add color, texture, or accents to your indoor space—small spaces can be uplifted, and large spaces warmed, by a few potted plants. You could try aloe vera, chillies, dwarf cumquat, mint, parsley, or pineapple.

When decorating your home, consider using edible plants as an alternative to cut flowers. At night, place a pot of lavender or a sweet-smelling herb such as thyme on a bedside table for yourself or a guest to drift into sleep with that lovely scent wafting through the air. Or how about arranging a table centerpiece for your next dinner party using potted microherbs and other edibles, and passing the scissors around to guests who can snip for themselves whichever greens they want on their plate? You can't get fresher than that.

There's nothing better than a relaxing bath after a hard day. Why not add some fresh herbs from nearby pots? I like rosemary and thyme for an invigorating bath, and lavender for a soothing bedtime bath.

Conditions

Growing edible plants indoors is not difficult, but you do need to understand your indoor environment, which needs a bit more maintenance than an outdoor garden.

- Track the movement of the sun in your house. All plants (except sprouts and mushrooms) need direct sunlight for a minimum of four hours a day.
- Understand the way that air moves through your home. Ideally, place plants where they will receive as much fresh air as possible.
- Make sure you have a handy water source and good access to the plants.
- Research the origins of edibles you'd like to try—can you reproduce their native habitats in your home?

Design

Moveable containers allow you to move plants from room to room to capture the sunlight. They are a great way to add color and design to your indoor space.

Choose materials, colors, and accents that suit your space and personal style. I wanted to bring a sense of the ocean into my home, so I incorporated blue Perspex planter boxes filled with herbs I use every day into my kitchen design (see page 62).

Tips and tricks

Here are a few tips to help keep your indoor edibles healthy:

- Place them where they will get enough direct sunlight.
- Rotate the plants 180 degrees every week.
- Use the best quality potting mix you can find.
- Repot perennials every one to two years, depending on the plant's growth rate.
- Water regularly, but don't overwater. If the soil is wet, don't water until it has dried out a little.
- Don't forget about proper drainage—if you get creative and plant in an old saucepan or teacup, remember to drill a hole in the bottom.
- Fertilize every two weeks with a liquid organic fertilizer. Combine this with a slow-release fertilizer designed specifically for indoor plants.
- Keep leaves clean by wiping with a damp cloth.
- If you can, take the plants outdoors occasionally for a spray with the hose. I suggest giving indoor edibles a three-day break outside every two weeks.
- Ensure good air circulation. Try to avoid drafts, as they will dry plants out very quickly.
- Keep an eye on pest and disease control.

IDEAL GROWING CONDITIONS FOR INDOOR EDIBLES

Full sun (6 hours of direct sunlight)

thyme	nasturtium
bay leaf	chamomile
oregano	borage
sage	chillies
rosemary	tomatoes
basil	

Partial sun (4 hours of direct sunlight)

parsley	peppermint
basil	chives
chervil	lettuce
mint	citrus

Low light (less than 4 hours to no sun)

sprouts	mushrooms

Some ideas to get you started

Growing herbs in pots on a sunny windowsill is a good place to start your indoor edible garden, but here are a few other creative options:

- **Mint in a hanging pot:** This plant is virtually unkillable! It doesn't need full sun to survive, so it's a great indoor edible. Plant mint in a hanging pot in an area of your home that gets morning sun and afternoon shade. Keep it moist and ensure good air circulation.

- **Instant spring onion forest:** Plant spring onions in a pot on a sunny windowsill and harvest as needed. Leave the base of the plant in the soil and it will resprout.

- **Potted pineapples:** Cut the top off a pineapple and leave it to dry for a day or so before planting into free-draining potting mix. Place in a bright spot with good air circulation. Be careful not to overwater or fertilize too much. Let the soil dry out between watering—pineapples don't like boggy soil.

- **Dwarf bananas:** Bananas are subtropical plants requiring lots of water, low light, and rich soil. Perfect for growing indoors! Not only do they provide edible fruit, but their bold leaves mean they look great as an accent plant. There is a range of dwarf banana varieties available.

RIVERPARK FARM

NEW YORK CITY

DELICIOUS GARDENS

This incredible urban farm sprang up on a 1675-square-yard vacant construction site in Manhattan over the spring and summer of 2012. It was developed by the owners of Riverpark Restaurant, which was right next door to the vacant site, and was made up of 7400 double-stacked milk crates planted with over 180 types of fruit, veggies, and herbs. These edibles provided fresh produce for the restaurant.

The Riverpark Farm team's approach to farming was sustainable, cost effective, and pretty funky. They used recycled milk crates because they're quick to install, reusable, and easy to turn into planters, and they chose crops they knew would thrive in crates.

The menu at Riverpark Restaurant was based on produce grown on the farm. Head chef and co-owner Sisha Ortúzar visited the farm daily to discuss with the gardeners what plants were ready to be harvested the following day. This is farm-to-table dining at its urban best.

Riverpark Farm has been hailed as a landmark example of urban farming. Not only did it provide local food, but the local community got involved, too, with over 1000 people visiting, many to help with the farming.

What's more, when construction was due to resume on the site, the farm team was able to pack up and move all the crates in under twenty-four hours. The farm has now reopened, not far away, and it continues to supply Riverpark Restaurant with a variety of produce, including salad greens, tomatoes, peppers, eggplants, cucumber, and berries.

Riverpark Farm's amazing contemporary (and moveable) farm made from old milk crates in the heart of New York City. It has over 180 different types of plants.

AT RIVERPARK FARM,
THE EDIBLES INCLUDE:

BEANS "GREEN TAVERA"

BORAGE

CARROTS "ATLAS"

CHAMOMILE

CHARD "BRIGHT LIGHTS"

CONCORD GRAPES

DILL

GIANT RED MUSTARD

GOLDEN BEETROOT

GROUND CHERRIES

LOVAGE

OKRA – RED

PURPLE MIZUNA

RADISHES "EASTER EGG"

RED SHISO

SQUASH "SAFARI"

SUGAR SNAP PEAS

TARRAGON

TATSOI

WATERCRESS

WATERMELONS

WILD MARJORAM

Q&A WITH SISHA ORTÚZAR

What inspired the design of this garden?
"The desire to grow our own produce for Riverpark Restaurant on a stalled construction site next door, while creating an attractive green space for our community in a spot that would otherwise be left vacant until development resumed."

What informed the plant selection for Riverpark Farm?
"We chose plants that we wanted to feature on our menus and that were likely to grow well in a cubic foot of soil in an urban environment. We also looked for plants with a high yield potential and ones that were difficult for us to source."

What has been the most surprising aspect of the garden?
"The response from our diners and the green-thumb community. We had support from the community in getting the project started, but were also excited to receive such interest from our diners, who would stop in before and after their visit to the restaurant to make those direct farm-to-table connections."

"We initiated community programs after receiving an overwhelming number of requests to visit and volunteer at the farm, and were thrilled to meet people of all ages and from all around the world who had heard about us and wanted to come and see the farm for themselves."

WHAT I LOVE ABOUT THIS DESIGN

- This garden of humble milk crates is very adaptable, and takes no more than a day to bump-in and bump-out if necessary.
- The simplicity of the containers and design—it is edgy, urban, and cool to look at, as well as practical.

YOU COULD DO THIS

This design is perfect for anyone wanting a temporary edible garden. It could be used for building sites, vacant lots, rented houses, and rooftops—the list goes on.

The team at Riverpark Farm lined their crates with a geotextile fabric (a specialized landscape fabric that keeps the soil in, but lets the water drain out). All you then need to do is to staple the liner to the top of the milk crate and fill with soil.

If you are thinking of building a moveable garden like this, choose materials that are transportable, lightweight, and stackable. Here are some ideas:

- Build planters on top of recycled timber pallets, with castors for moving.
- Fill up old coffee bags with soil and grow some veggies in them. When the bags start to break down, just add them to your compost heap.
- Olive oil tins make great lightweight vegetable pots. Be careful when cutting the top off, and make sure you fold the sharp edge over so as not to cut fingers. Don't forget to pierce holes in the bottom for drainage.
- Use apple crates.

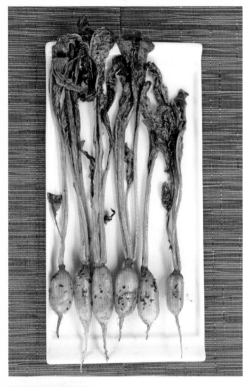

Sisha Ortúzar and Jeffrey Zurofsky discussing the daily farm-to-table menu.

There are no food miles here, just fresh, wholesome goodness.

The Kershaw family

Robbie and Elena, and their children Lulu and Kofi, have a thriving edible garden.

There are vegetable garden beds everywhere—planter boxes, raised beds, wicking beds, bathtubs, and potted plants. There is even produce growing in the narrow strip of earth between the driveway and the house—corn, cucumber, chard, spinach, various salad crops, and tomatoes.

Some espaliered apple and orange trees in the front yard provide screening, while others shade the house. They're interspersed with camellia shrubs and edibles such as rhubarb and celery.

Although the plot of land is quite small, there are more than ten fruit trees, including apple, cool banana, orange, lemon, mandarin, and a kaffir lime. A good portion of the garden beds is dedicated to herbs: basil, rosemary, mint, Vietnamese mint, thyme, sage, oregano, chives, coriander, lemon grass, and dill.

The garden includes two aquaponics systems, which contain over one hundred rainbow trout in two tanks, and feed two grow beds packed with vegetables (for more on aquaponics, see pages 186–87).

This family is the very model of environmental awareness. Robbie's motto is: "If it once lived, it can go in the compost." So everything from kitchen scraps to prunings from the garden is composted. To top it all off, they have a small chicken coop in the backyard, which holds five bantam chickens that lay enough eggs through the warmer months to keep the family going.

CHAPTER THREE
VERTICAL GARDENS

Pushing your edible garden up the wall maximizes not only your growing space, but also your overall living space. Just like a veggie patch in your garden, you can design your edible wall to best suit you and your space. From a traditional espalier to the more contemporary designs we are now seeing in cities, it's time to grow up.

WHAT'S IT ALL ABOUT?

—— Vertical gardens have been instrumental in changing the way we approach garden design, encouraging us to think outside the square, and sparking some incredible innovations. Space is always going to be one of our most precious commodities and you can't get a better solution to maximizing green space, and living space, than the vertical garden concept. It's a clever way to expand greenery in a small space, soften hard architecture, cover up unattractive fences or walls, and enclose or divide areas.

Even better, a wall of edibles lets you grow produce wherever you like. Imagine plucking salad greens from the wall next to your outdoor dining table, or herbs for your cup of tea while kicking back on a deckchair in your courtyard. That's what I really love about vertical gardens—they bring the garden to you. You're encouraged to use the produce because it's on display, unlike the forgotten veggie patch at the bottom of the garden, or the herbs you hardly ever use because they're too far from the kitchen.

When you're planning a vertical garden, there are three ways to go about it. The easiest option is to pay a professional greenwall company to install one for you. If you choose this route, make sure the wall is tailored to your requirements, that there is sufficient irrigation and drainage, and that the plants are suitable for your climate and purposes. The second option is to buy prefabricated panels that can be attached to a wall, fence, or frame. Lastly, you can go the DIY route, filling a timber or metal shelving system with a variety of plants in pots, or simply setting up a trellis system to espalier suitable plants. It can be as simple (and cheap) or elaborate (and expensive) as you like. The end result will be the same—a beautiful and useful wall of vegetation.

When you're choosing your plants, think about how they will come together once in place—having a few spillover plants, such as prostrate rosemary, will help to minimize bald patches.

Once it's set up, a vertical garden requires no special attention, although regular fertilizing and watering are a must. If you've used potting mix, you should change it every year or two, depending on the greenwall system you've put in place. Now that you're ready to go, here are some sources of inspiration that I hope will spark your creativity.

A stunning vertical garden designed by Patrick Blanc for fellow vertical gardener, Noémie Vialard, in Brittany, France. It is filled with edible aromatic plants.

PATRICK BLANC

One of the pioneers of vertical gardening, Patrick Blanc started constructing green walls in France in the late 1990s and has since become internationally renowned, with projects all over the world. His creation of the Vertical Garden (Mur Végétal) has totally transformed the possibilities of what a garden can be, offering remarkable solutions for public buildings and urban gardens.

A botanist who became an artist at the age of fifty-two, Patrick took everything he knew about plants and used it to transform his plantings into vertical art. He understands what plants really need and this knowledge gives him the freedom to experiment with gardens that seem to defy gravity. Plants "glue" themselves to whatever will sustain them, so all Patrick has done is to create the right conditions for healthy plant growth on the sides of buildings or other walls. Once a waterproof membrane is in place to prevent moisture seeping into the wall, cushions of sponge-like fabric are attached. This horticultural material allows for the free flow of air, nutrients, water, and trace elements—it's almost like upholstering the wall—and is thick enough for the roots to grow through. Over time, the roots take over, becoming the new transportation system for water and nutrients.

Patrick draws his inspiration from natural environments where plants and landforms grow vertically, such as epiphytes (plants that grow on the branches and trunks of trees, deriving all they need from the surrounding air) and inselbergs (the isolated rocky outcrops that naturally occur within a landscape), as well as the architecture of leaf colors, waterfalls, root systems, and plants that find their way into the cracks and corners of buildings and rock faces. With a focus on texture and forms, the gardens Patrick creates are truly inspirational.

WHO OR WHAT INSPIRES ME?

I had the pleasure of meeting the master of vertical wall gardens himself, Patrick Blanc, in Paris. Inspirational. He is one of the most energetic and creative men I've ever met. He has green everything—hair, fingernails, and clothes!

EDIBLE GREEN WALL, ATLANTA BOTANICAL GARDEN, GEORGIA, USA

In 2010, a parking lot right in the center of midtown Atlanta was transformed into an incredible green space, with a curved edible green wall enclosing three garden "rooms" and an outdoor kitchen. The $2 million project demonstrates the city's commitment to environmentally sensitive gardening, and to promoting and supporting local, sustainable produce. A 10,500 gallon underground water tank was installed to take care of the watering needs of a large amount of the garden.

The wall itself is about 52 feet long and 8 feet high, consisting of over one hundred modules overflowing with around 2000 edible plants, mainly aromatic herbs. I can only imagine how much planning and research went into the selection of plants that would thrive in the Atlanta climate and need minimal maintenance. It's the most remarkable achievement, and I take my hat off to everyone involved.

In contrast to Patrick Blanc's "wild and woolly" green walls, this one is neatly trimmed and clipped close to the wall, so you really get a sense of all the diverse textures and vibrant greens of the vegetation. It's composed of a series of clip-on plastic modules containing small planters that are only about 6 inches, arranged diagonally, and the beauty of this system is that you can clip each one out individually, making it very versatile. Together the modules create a sweeping curve, like a speakeasy wall where you whisper at one end and it echoes at the other.

To stand in the encircling arm of herbs and vegetables, the air fragrant with rosemary and thyme, is an amazing sensory experience.

DESIGNING WITH VERTICALS

I've always felt that gardens should be plentiful, especially if the plants grown in them are edible. That wonderful sense of abundance is paramount. So when it comes to planting a vertical edible garden wall, it is vital that you choose plants that suit your zone and season.

Just as important is a good knowledge of the plants' habits. You may want to grow plants that have dense foliage or are lateral spreaders. Or even better, those with a spillover habit like prostrate rosemary. Vertical gardens look terrible with bald spots, so choosing appropriate plants ensures that foliage covers any gaps.

DOWN AND DIRTY

Creating green walls

- **Exposure:** How much sun does the wall receive? This will obviously have a huge impact on which plants will grow well in your vertical garden. For example, north-facing walls retain a lot of heat, so choose plants that are heat-tolerant, and bear in mind that exposure to sun and wind will dry out the soil faster.

- **Feeding:** The type of vertical garden, its exposure and plant varieties, will determine how much water and fertilizer you'll need to keep the garden looking good.

- **Maintenance:** How will you maintain your vertical garden? Is it easy to replace plants or fix the irrigation system if it breaks? Make sure you install a vertical garden you are comfortable with and understand.

- **Materials:** There are various ways you can approach this, depending on your budget. You can hire a professional greenwall company to install a vertical garden for you, or you can buy prefabricated panels to attach to a frame or existing wall yourself. If you're on a tight budget, get creative with found objects, hanging pots, climbing plants, and so on.

- **Layout:** Personally, I like the way Patrick Blanc creates his green walls on the diagonal, which feels more naturalistic. A vertical arrangement, with defined rows of crops, is best for people who want to harvest straight from the wall, while a more random layout suits a mixture of ornamental and edible plantings.

ZONING YOUR VERTICAL GARDEN

I am passionate about smart planting design—this means not only selecting plants appropriate for the conditions, but also placing them where they will be useful. This applies to all types of gardens, including green walls. The location of your green wall should be influenced by function, which will also affect the type of edibles used in it.

Here are some plant-zoning ideas for your vertical garden:

- **Outdoor kitchen:** Cultivate plants that can go directly from the garden to your table, such as basil, parsley, spinach, microherbs, and lettuce.

- **Outdoor lounge room:** Select plants that can be used in drinks, such as lemon verbena, basil, and mint.

- **Outdoor bathing:** Choose fragrant and nurturing edible plants, such as peppermint, lavender, and geranium.

GOOD EDIBLE PLANT CHOICES FOR VERTICAL GARDENS

As long as your growing medium is free-draining and allows the flow of water, nutrients, and air, you can pretty much grow anything on a vertical surface. Here are some suggestions as a starting point:

basil	parsley
beans	peas
chives	prostrate rosemary
lettuce	sage
marjoram	sorrel
mint	spinach
nasturtiums	strawberries
oregano	thyme

Some ideas to get you started

Over the last decade, there has been significant interest in vertical gardens as a way of bringing nature into harsh city environments, and the range of different systems has really expanded. Creating a vertical garden really can be as simple or as complicated as you like. Here are some creative, low-tech vertical garden ideas that won't break the bank:

- **Ladder:** Rest an old wooden ladder against the wall and place potted plants on the rungs. You could also grow a climbing plant up the ladder—try passion fruit, runner beans, or sweet potatoes.

- **Shelving system with terracotta pots:** Reuse an industrial-style timber or metal shelving system or build one yourself and use it to support a range of edible plants in pots. Just like a plant bookshelf!

- **Hanging plants:** I love the look of a wall of plants that are hanging down from the ceiling, rather than growing up from the ground. Spillover plants such as prostrate rosemary grown in hanging pots create a wonderful green curtain.

HOW TO ESPALIER

Espaliering is the art of growing a tree or shrub, in a flat form, along a wall or frame. It's a great way of fitting lots of edibles and foliage into a small space and creating a striking feature at the same time. The technique can be used on a range of edible plants, including citrus, apples, pears, olives, figs, and pomegranates. The best species to choose will depend on your climate, space, and site conditions.

Here are some tips:

- **Select your location:** As a general rule, most fruit-producing plants require good drainage, plenty of sun, and protection from strong winds.

- **Establish a framework:** It's essential to have a sturdy frame to tie the branches to when training an espalier. If using wire, make sure it is tensioned, can take some weight, and is attached securely to a wall or frame. Space the wires about 12 inches apart.

- **Species selection:** Which edible trees will work best pretty much boils down to your location and climate. Do your research and ask at your local nursery if you need a little extra advice. Espaliering is a long-term project and it is crucial to start with an appropriate plant species, otherwise you will just be wasting precious time and money.

- **Plant selection:** Once you have decided what type of tree you want to grow, it's time to choose the individual plant from a nursery. Make sure it has good structure, a strong, straight trunk, and a relatively symmetrical branch structure. Look for plants that can be trained easily in a horizontal manner.

- **Planting:** Once you have your structure ready and have prepared and enriched your soil with organic matter and compost, it's time to plant. Place the edible tree as close to the structure as possible. Prune all branches that cannot be trained to grow along the framework and tie all branches that can be trained to the wires or frame with flexible ties.

- **Pruning:** Espaliers need regular maintenance, including pruning over the growing season, to ensure good structure.

GROWING MEDIUMS FOR VERTICAL GARDENS

Most vertical systems use a lightweight potting mix rather than soil. Wet soil is very heavy and can compromise the structure of a vertical garden, and it may not drain freely enough. Of course it all depends on the individual garden. Some are based on small pockets cut into layers of felt and hardly need any growing medium at all; others use pots filled with potting mix. Essentially, the growing medium required will be determined by the vertical garden system you've decided on. A few basic principles apply, though:

- **Nutrients:** Vertical gardens generally need more fertilizing than regular gardens because there aren't as many nutrients in the growing medium. Some vertical garden designs will deliver fertilizer via an irrigation system, while other designs need you to supply fertilizer by hand or as a slow-release fertilizer within the growing medium.
- **Drainage:** Like container gardens, vertical gardens need good drainage.
- **Weight:** Use a lightweight potting mix.
- **Longevity:** Potting mix does not last forever. Remember that you will have to change the mix every one to two years, depending on the soil type and greenwall system you choose.

OUTDOOR DINING ROOM

DELICIOUS GARDENS

LOS ANGELES

Tucked away in suburban Los Angeles is a dining room with a difference. First, it's outdoors; second, it's surrounded on three sides by the "walls" of an extravagant edible vertical garden. I designed this garden for a couple, Jennifer and Scott, as part of *The Outdoor Room* television series. They were great clients who were passionate about growing and eating their own food. One of the first things Jennifer said to me was, "If I can't eat it, I don't want it in my garden." What a great design instruction!

Jennifer and Scott felt overwhelmed by the size and emptiness of the yard. They didn't know where to start, but knew it had to be productive. Jennifer mentioned to me that she felt like their property ended at the back door. When I heard this, I knew I had to expand their home into their back garden, so it would become a place they wanted to spend time in. Basically, I wanted to make them feel as if their garden was simply an extension of their kitchen.

After discussing their needs and desires with them, I found myself remembering the inspiring design of the Atlanta Botanical Garden, especially the huge edible green wall (see pages 86-87). I decided to create a similar style of vertical garden for Jennifer and Scott, albeit a little smaller in scale. My plan was to create a sense of enclosure within an outdoor dining area, while also providing more edible growing space in their garden.

This inspiration, combined with the clients' wishes, formed the basis for a contemporary garden design with a timber-framed dining pavilion at its heart. Large timber pontoons connect the pavilion with the rest of the garden and meander through the vegetable garden and down into the orchard at the back of the space.

The finished product contains almost fifty edibles, many used in the vertical garden surrounding the dining pavilion. The orchard at the rear of the yard has orange, lemon, peach, pear, and plum trees, plus a range of ornamental plantings for year-round interest and structure, and enough space to grow vegetables for continuous supply through the year. This really is an edible paradise.

The timber-framed dining pavilion with vertical pockets filled with edible plants gives a sense of enclosure and intimacy that is perfect for entertaining family and friends.

JENNIFER AND SCOTT GROW THE FOLLOWING IN THEIR OUTDOOR DINING ROOM:

BASIL

BROCCOLI

CAULIFLOWER

CHAMOMILE

CHARD

COLLARD GREENS

DILL

FIGS

GARLIC CHIVES

KALE

LEMONS

LEMON GRASS

LETTUCES

NASTURTIUMS

ONION CHIVES

ORANGES

OREGANO

PARSLEY

PEACHES

PEARS

PLUMS

ROSEMARY

SAGE

SORREL

THYME

VIOLETS

WILD STRAWBERRIES

WINTER ZUCCHINI

Q&A WITH JENNIFER

What do you like to do in your new garden?
"We can have breakfast and dinner in our new dining room, or bring our laptops out here. We read the paper and relax—it's really nice. It's also a great place to entertain."

What's been the biggest surprise?
"The back of the house feels so much better—it's like a whole other living area out here. The amount of produce we get from the garden is amazing. We wouldn't have imagined having a vertical veggie garden before this."

Are you happy with your new garden?
"We love it. It's hard to believe that it really is our garden, not someone else's!"

WHAT I LOVE ABOUT THIS DESIGN

- **Simplicity:** This garden is all about simple structure, a minimal palette of materials and plenty of plants.
- **Shelter and protection:** Having an all-weather dining pavilion means that plenty of time can be spent outdoors, regardless of the weather.
- **Space:** This garden uses all the available space for edible plants. It is a great example of making the most of a suburban lot to grow your own food.
- **Convenience:** The vertical garden wall in the dining area makes it possible to just lean over and pick leaves or garnishes to add your meal at the dining table—how cool is that?

YOU COULD DO THIS

Jennifer and Scott's garden is based on a simple, modern layout. It is divided into three sections by low concrete retaining walls and is accessed via a central pathway of pontoons and gravel. We pressed flat stones into the face of the concrete, which helped to turn utilitarian retaining walls into objects of beauty.

The first things to determine when designing a similar garden are the proportions of the different spaces, how high the retaining walls need to be (if necessary), and where to position the dining pavilion. As a rule, I prefer to place entertaining areas as close to the house as possible, as they will be used much more if they are easily accessible.

Once the structure is designed and you have a clear plan, consider the materials you will use within the garden. Here, we used lots of timber and painted it dark green to make it feel completely integrated. If you are planning on painting timber for your garden, it may be more cost effective and easier to use primed pine rather than hardwood.

Throughout the design process, we used sustainable urban-gardening practices. The vertical living wall planters, which we hung on a simple timber frame, are made of a non-biodegradable material produced from recycled plastic bottles.

What really makes a garden special are the personal touches—they transform a blank canvas into a warm, individual destination infused with the personality of the owner. Draw on color themes from your home or from flowers in your garden and incorporate these into cushions, lights, furniture, and decorative objects. Remember, it's much easier to change the color of a cushion than that of an entire boundary wall.

ENCLOSURE WITH EDIBLES

One of the most important features of any successful garden is privacy. This can be achieved through built structures, such as fences, walls, and pergolas; or through vertical plantings, using hedges, climbers on a trellis, or trees. Here is a list of some of the best edible plants for creating an enclosure:

- **Bay tree:** Great in cooler climates for an edible hedge. The leaves (fresh or dried) are widely used for flavoring dishes such as casseroles, sauces, and curries.
- **Tea:** This very slow-growing plant makes a great hedge, providing both privacy and one of the world's favorite drinks—tea!
- **Passion fruit:** Train a couple of these plants to grow up a trellis and you will have a dense green screen, beautiful sculptural flowers, and delicious fruit. Just make sure you have more than one vine, as passion fruit is monoecious (this means that each plant is either male or female and requires a plant of the other gender nearby for pollination).
- **Kiwifruit:** This climbing plant is well suited to creating edible privacy screens in cooler areas. It is monoecious, like passion fruit.
- **Walnut:** This deciduous tree makes a seriously amazing roof for an outdoor entertaining area in cooler climates. Its dense leaves provide shade in the warmer months, but it loses its leaves in winter so you get the warmth of the sun. Walnut trees grow best in temperate climates and do need a bit of space, as they develop quite a broad canopy as they mature.
- **Olive tree:** Although they are fairly slow growing, olive trees are very hardy, especially in dry climates with minimal humidity. Within around seven years, you could have a crop of olives, too.

VERTICAL GARDEN

LOS ANGELES

DELICIOUS GARDENS

When I first met Samantha and Seth Barnes, their young daughter Cecily, and their golden retriever Auggie it didn't take long for us to work out a highly practical edible garden design. Samantha is the cofounder of Kitchen Kid, a mobile cooking school that teaches local kids how to cook, and the family wanted to integrate their family space with a workshop where Samantha could teach.

I wanted to design an outdoor space that would extend the family's living area and would also feature a productive garden. I also wanted to create a variety of living spaces, including a parents' retreat, an entertaining area, and some lawn for Cecily and her friends to run around on.

The design solution was to create a number of outdoor rooms in one backyard by using an A-frame to grow fresh food. We installed a set of concertina doors in the living room wall to connect the home's interior to a new deck. Using recycled material and furnishings, we transformed the old garage into a classroom for the Kitchen Kid students. We built a stone-floored patio next to the classroom, a pergola for resting or dining, and a walkway to connect the new deck with the kitchen classroom.

We brought the yard to life with a vertical garden that would produce enough fruit, herbs, and vegetables to feed the family, as well as the Kitchen Kid students—we planted over forty edibles. For the kids to interact well with the garden, I knew they would need easy access, so I created vertical garden wall pockets sitting on low A-frames, with plants spilling out on both sides. This meant that the plants on the lower levels weren't overshadowed by the higher plants, resulting in much higher yields.

Last, but not least, we built an outdoor parents' retreat with a raised fire pit for Samantha and Seth, and we placed a blanket of lawn for young Cecily to play on in clear view of the house, deck, and parents' retreat.

SAMANTHA AND SETH'S
EDIBLE GARDEN INCLUDES:

BASIL

BLACKBERRIES

BLUEBERRIES

BROCCOLI

CAPSICUMS

CARROTS

CHIVES

CORIANDER

CUMQUATS

FIGS

GLOBE ARTICHOKES

GRAPES

KALE

LETTUCES

MARJORAM

MINT

OREGANO

PARSLEY

ROSEMARY

SAGE

STRAWBERRIES

THYME

TOMATOES

ZUCCHINI

Q&A WITH SAMANTHA BARNES

What's your favorite thing to do in the garden?
"I love sitting out by the fire. In the evening, it's a great place to unwind with a glass of wine and some good company."

Who is responsible for keeping the garden alive?
"My husband and I, plus a gardener who comes weekly. I can't wait until Cecily is old enough to help out!"

Biggest lesson learned from the garden transformation?
"Jamie did incredible things with an ordinary backyard—he created so many unique, multipurpose, and beautiful outdoor rooms."

WHAT I LOVE ABOUT THIS DESIGN

The A-frame structure is an ergonomic design that is accessible for children and anyone less mobile, as it makes watering, picking, and plant maintenance easier. Space-savvy design means you can plant on both sides of the frame.

The beauty of these A-frames is that they're mobile, making them a good option for renters, and they're adaptable enough to work almost anywhere: on a balcony, in a courtyard, or lined up in multiples in a larger garden. They can be moved around the garden to take advantage of seasonal conditions, or repositioned to establish new outdoor room layouts.

The A-frame concept works perfectly to divide spaces and line pathways, leading people through a garden and making use of otherwise potentially "dead" space.

YOU COULD DO THIS

To create this garden, first you need to build or buy your A-frames. Structures can be purpose-built for an exact fit, or installed in sections to allow maximum flexibility. How many structures to have will be determined by both the size of your space and your ambitions. You might want to start big, or consider adding structures as your passion grows. Multiple structures can look great lining both sides of a path or used as dividers to create different zones throughout the garden.

When deciding where to place your structures, have a think about the following:

- Where does light fall in your garden through the seasons?

- How can the structure be used for added functionality—to direct people through the garden, divide an area, or make use of an otherwise unused space?

- How accessible is this positioning for planting, watering, picking, and maintenance needs?

- Finally, what edibles do you want to grow, and what are their growing needs?

HOW TO GET KIDS INTERESTED IN COOKING AND EATING THE FRUITS (AND VEGGIES) OF YOUR LABOR

One of the things I love most about getting kids involved in a veggie garden is that they start wanting to eat what they grow! While creating her garden, Samantha shared with me her tried and tested tips for encouraging kids to cook and eat veggies from the garden:

- Kids as young as three or four can help in the kitchen. Give them a pair of blunt craft scissors for snipping herbs such as basil.

- Kids can count out the number of ingredients you need, and measure quantities using cups and spoons—they love to count and it helps with their math, too!

- Kids who help with the cooking are much more likely to eat what they've made. Commit to spending one night a week cooking dinner with your kids. Happily, they often like the prep work that parents don't: drying lettuce, peeling carrots, and grating cheese.

- A kitchen is filled with flavors from all over the world; encourage an interest in different cultures and geography by putting up a world map and using pins to show where your family's favorite recipes come from.

ERGONOMIC DESIGN

Ergonomic design is extremely important to make your garden functional. Before applying shovel to dirt or hammer to nail, consider who tends your garden, and what their individual needs are. How high or low can people bend or reach? Should there be smooth walkways through the space to allow for wheelchairs or easy access? Do you need somewhere to put your tools? How will you water? The more comfortable your garden is for you and your helpers, the more enjoyable the time spent tending it will be!

SUCCESS STORIES

Cromer Community Center

I recently completed a makeover of the garden at this Center, which is used by more than thirty local groups, including playgroups, sporting groups, church groups, and others. My aim was to create a low-maintenance, functional garden integrating hardy edibles with ornamentals. I wanted to create defined spaces that could be used by different groups at the same time, and a place where people would want to spend time.

We planted lemon and cumquat trees, created three raised planter beds, blending rosemary hedges with artichoke feature plants, and built a contemporary veggie garden, using coreten steel planters to grow herbs including thyme, rosemary, oregano, and lemon grass.

My favorite feature is the 82-foot vertical garden, which has one panel that is almost entirely planted with edibles including marjoram, red cabbage, garlic, broad beans, blueberries, kiwifruit, leeks, and strawberries. It looks amazing, and the produce will be available to anyone who uses the space.

There is one aspect of this story I really love. One of the Center's main users is the Link Church, which runs a "shop" where people in need can buy groceries at subsidized prices and get free fruit and vegetables as well. It won't be long before that will include produce from the Center's own garden. It doesn't get better than that.

CHAPTER FOUR

THE KITCHEN GARDEN REINVENTED

The kitchen garden is getting a modern makeover. It's all about mixing everything up to suit your space and needs. You can make it traditional or contemporary—but most importantly, make it your own by integrating all the things you love.

—— Kitchen gardens are back in vogue, thanks to the organic food movement, a desire for sustainability and the rising costs of produce. Even the White House has an organic veggie patch, set up by the Obamas in 2009 to be used for their family meals. Michelle Obama's reason for donning the gardening gloves was to encourage her children to eat more nutritious foods, and she's also involved in raising awareness to combat the problem of childhood obesity. As part of her "Let's Move" campaign, which aims to raise a healthier generation of kids, the First Lady recently joined students from all over America to harvest the White House Kitchen Garden's summer crop.

This is the great advantage of kitchen gardens—not only do they provide food, they also provide a reason to go outdoors and dig, weed, compost, and harvest. They teach children about the source of food and are fantastic educational tools. Kids learn to nurture and respect nature, simply by having the opportunity to scratch around in the dirt and look at what's going on around them.

My appreciation for the kitchen garden started with the one we had at home when I was a boy. I was lucky enough to grow up with an abundance of fresh produce on our doorstep—the garden was Mum's pride and joy, and her Sri Lankan heritage was a big influence on what she grew and how we ate it. The immense pleasure she gets from tending her garden and cooking whatever is in season (and sharing it with everyone she knows!) goes to show how the simple act of growing food can enrich our lives in so many ways (see pages 124–31 for the story of Mama Durie's garden).

A successful kitchen garden doesn't have to be large—you'll reap the rewards of growing even a few herbs and veggies. Once you've experienced the satisfaction of eating homegrown produce, though, it's hard to resist planting more. My most vivid memory of taking something out of the ground, cooking it, and eating it was on a beach holiday with friends. They were growing potatoes and I dug some up, threw them into a saucepan, and ran down to the surf to fill it up with seawater. We boiled them and ate them with dobs of butter and freshly ground black pepper—I can still recall the amazing flavor of those spuds. There is nothing quite like the taste of food straight out of the soil, and that's why growing edibles is so addictive. Before you know it, you'll be composting, seeking out heirloom seeds, and installing a chicken coop!

WHY "REINVENTED"?

I thought I'd include a short explanation of why I've called this chapter "The Kitchen Garden Reinvented." Traditional kitchen gardens were hidden at the far end of the backyard and originated from the need to grow fresh produce for the family table. Kitchen gardens of today are still, of course, used to grow produce, but they have had an image makeover. These days, people don't just want their gardens to produce food; they want them to look good, too. Because of that, kitchen gardens are now proudly displayed and a lot of thought goes into their design. Color, texture, height, and even planting combinations are far more considered than they once were. Kitchen gardens are well maintained and form an integral part of the overall garden design, and they are as attractive as they are practical.

In a modern kitchen garden, raised planter beds might have edging that doubles as seating. Stepping stones may meander through the garden beds, with an ornamental and practical purpose, since they make it easier to maintain the garden. Different plants, such as kale and beet, might be grown together and used to frame the garden borders and also to add vibrant color to the bed. Canopy trees, such as bay or even pineapple guava, could be clipped into topiaries, or pleached hedges into ornamental shapes that help create microclimates for the plants below. Ornamental bowls spill over with strawberries, fruit trees double as privacy hedges, and edible climbing trellises shaped into pyramids or obelisks give structure, verticality, and architecture. Apple trees may be espaliered across walls to provide an edible landscape as well as decoration.

These are just a handful of ideas, invented centuries ago, that DIY gardeners of today are now embracing, as much from a design perspective as a produce perspective.

There is a groundswell going on that is design-led—the produce is an added bonus. The kitchen garden that was once hidden has now become integrated and is often a focal point. Kitchen gardens have become cool! The function of modern landscaping so far has primarily been focused on adding visual interest and a lovely natural form to our outdoor spaces, but finally the trend of integrating edibles is going in the direction of adding substance as well. The beautiful thing about growing food today is that it's about both nutrition and design, so we never have to be ashamed of the veggie patch again. Gotta love that.

ALICE WATERS

Alice Waters' food philosophy can be summed up in four words: fresh, seasonal, local, and sustainable. And nothing demonstates her commitment to this more than her restaurant, Chez Panisse, in Berkeley, California, where a trusted community of sustainable food producers, farmers, and artisans have been supplying Alice with ingredients for more than forty years. Think about that—forty years! This woman was way ahead of her time.

Back in 1996, Alice created the Edible Schoolyard model to teach school children about nature's food cycles. Her motivation was to instil in them the knowledge and values needed to build a fair and sustainable future, and to teach them to respect the food they eat and, by extension, the planet they live on. The program, which has since evolved into The Edible Schoolyard Project, was such a success that it led to the School Lunch Initiative, designed to teach children in public schools across America about nutrition and gardening, and the obvious connection between the two.

I love the way Alice thinks, and I love the way she cares so deeply about the world around her and will fight tooth and nail to protect it. I once had the pleasure of meeting and interviewing her about homegrown food. She is the Vice President of Slow Food International, so it came as no surprise that she really knows her stuff, and the passion with which she shares it is infectious. Ever since, I have been watching with delight as the world slowly falls back in love with the vegetable patch.

WHO OR WHAT INSPIRES ME?

THE URBAN HOMESTEAD, PASADENA

Jules Dervaes and his family have created a unique place that is paving the way for what I call a future farm. The Urban Homestead is a successful, sustainable working model that combines all the elements of a small farm: a productive food garden, small livestock, and beekeeping. Visiting the homestead in Pasadena, just fifteen minutes from downtown Los Angeles, was an incredible experience.

It all began in the mid-1980s, when Jules started reading about genetically modified corn. He decided to start growing his own food so that he would know exactly what was in it and where it was coming from. But rather than simply adding a few edibles to his existing plants, he decided to go all out. "We grow over 350 different vegetables, herbs, fruits, and berries in a garden that is 395 square yards, harvesting an average of 6000 pounds of produce every year," he tells me, as we wander among healthy plants laden with fresh produce.

By making our backyards more productive, as the Dervaes have done, we are helping both ourselves and the planet. Global population is increasing at such a rate that we need to find innovative ways to put food on the family table. Jamie Oliver calls it "The Food Revolution" and Jules Dervaes is one of the original revolutionaries. By turning private gardens into alternative food sources we regain control over the food that goes into our mouths and we reconnect with the cycles of nature.

The Dervaes family's Urban Homestead is a shining example of this philosophy in action and I'm a huge fan. They provide inspiration for the rest of us to cultivate the earth and produce food for ourselves.

STONEFIELDS
DAYLESFORD REGION, VICTORIA

DELICIOUS GARDENS

Stonefields is one of Australia's premier rural gardens. Owned by renowned landscape designer Paul Bangay, the seven-acre garden illustrates his passion for balance, restraint and elegance, and of course, edible gardening. I think Paul is one of the greatest designers of our time. I first met him in the years before I started my garden design business. He has been by far my greatest mentor; he put me on the path that I am still on today, which began with studying horticulture and led to fifteen years of travelling the world—an incredible journey inspired by his work.

What I take away from Paul's design sense is his innate ability to create drama. He helps us appreciate the beauty in every plant by defining the space and framing it with his impeccable plant choice. He's a bit like a shepherd, guiding our journey through his gardens with his carefully considered designs.

Paul says, 'Over the past few years I've travelled extensively around England and Europe, focusing mainly on vegetable and productive gardens. My own garden is greatly inspired by these travels, as I learnt that they have much to teach us about sustainable garden design. I was particularly influenced by Victorian and Edwardian English vegetable gardens developed to service large estates.'

The beauty of the Stonefields veggie garden is in its pared-back, yet still formal, design. Built out of little more than recycled timber and gravel, it's successful because of its relationship to the rest of the garden and its uncomplicated, elegant structure. And if you love the edible part of Paul's garden you've just got to see the rest—his latest book, *The Garden at Stonefields*, is one of the best he's ever produced.

I love the way Paul has framed the low rectangular garden beds with a tall cypress hedge to create a microclimate, and has used plants like fennel to soften the overall design as well as for their edibility.

HERE ARE SOME OF THE EDIBLES PAUL GROWS IN HIS STUNNING INTEGRATED GARDEN:

APPLES 'CRIMSON CRISP'

BLACK CURRANTS

BROAD BEANS

BROCCOLI

CARROTS 'ST. VALERY'

CELERIAC

FIGS 'BLACK GENOA'

HEIRLOOM TOMATOES

LETTUCE 'ITALIAN LOLLO'

PLUMS 'SANTA ROSA'

POMEGRANATES

POTATOES 'ROYAL BLUE' AND 'DUTCH CREAM'

RASPBERRIES

RED CURRANTS

RHUBARB 'WANDIN GIANT' AND 'EVER RED'

STRAWBERRIES 'RED GAUNTLET'

Q&A WITH PAUL BANGAY

What was the driving force behind creating an edible garden at Stonefields?
'Ever since I was a child, I have always had my own vegetable garden. I strongly believe in the power and benefits of growing your own produce and I've tried to make Stonefields as sustainable as possible. We have vegetables, herbs, meat in the form of cattle, eggs, honey from our own hives and fruit from the many fruit trees I've planted.'

What is your favorite time of day in the garden and why?
'Early morning, when I go down to collect the eggs and water the vegetable garden. The birds are so vocal and the rest of the garden is so still and void of activity. I feel as if I have the whole garden to myself.'

What was the best surprise?
'I planted beds for the long-term, using edibles such as asparagus and currants (black and red). These have now come to fruition and there is nothing better than harvesting fresh asparagus spears or making jam from your own red currants.'

What is your favourite edible plant and why?
'Rhubarb! I have discovered a very old and sweet variety, which I grow in terracotta forcing pots I had made; these force the stalks up so they become sweeter.'

WHAT I LOVE ABOUT THIS DESIGN

When I heard Paul was creating his own veggie patch I knew it would be something special, and it certainly lived up to my expectations. This stunning vegetable garden reflects the structure of the rest of the Stonefields garden, using boundary hedges, the symmetrical layout of beds, and simple material selection. This gives the spaces a real connection and provides continuity within the design.

Some of my favourite features of the vegetable garden at Stonefields include:

- The way Paul puts structure around whimsical beauty—just look at the combination of a low box hedge with tall bay and the feathery foliage of fennel. The low rectangular beds are framed by a tall cypress hedge and incorporate low pomegranate hedges, woven willow borders, rhubarb pots, and pea trellises. Low box hedges border his herbs, and plants such as sage and fennel are used as much for their good looks as their edibility.

- Perennial edibles, such as asparagus, gooseberries, and rhubarb, have been integrated to provide year-round interest and a sense of abundance.

- The garden is susceptible to attack by the local wildlife, especially rabbits, and Paul solved this problem by harvesting willow branches from a tree on his property and weaving a low 'rabbit-proof fence'. I love this fence— as well as being a practical pest-control measure, its rustic, handmade appearance tempers the formal design of the garden.

- All the materials used in the garden were sourced locally—some from Stonefields itself, including the timber that edges the garden beds. The gravel around the beds is from a quarry down the road. It's a wonderful example of how to create a beautiful, formal, and elegant space using sustainable, local materials.

YOU COULD DO THIS

A highly structured layout like this is best suited to a formal garden design. Symmetry is very important, so if you do decide to try this, first draw up a plan to ensure the space is balanced. If in doubt, keep it simple.

Using locally sourced materials is great for the environment and usually cheaper, too. Making use of recycled or renewable objects from your own property is the ultimate in sustainable gardening!

As I've said before, well-prepared soil is the most important element of any edible garden, so it's worth making the effort to improve yours if necessary. Paul undertook extensive earthworks before installing his garden, but most soils will simply need composting, improved drainage or a better pH balance.

STEPHANIE ALEXANDER KITCHEN GARDEN FOUNDATION

Paul Bangay sits on the board of the Stephanie Alexander Kitchen Garden Foundation, offering his considerable knowledge and experience to help this amazing organization prosper and grow. Established by Stephanie Alexander OAM in 2004, the Kitchen Garden Program teaches kids all about food production, from preparing garden beds to planting out seeds, harvesting ripe produce, and even preparing it to eat.

From its humble beginnings at just one school in Melbourne, the program is now up and running in roughly 300 primary schools around Australia. It's enormously successful, and it's easy to see why. Kids are involved in the process from start to finish. They're getting their hands dirty (under teacher's orders!) and watching seedlings shoot up and grow into plants ready to harvest.

They are learning how to nurture the plants and how to tell what's ripe for picking. Then they take their produce into the kitchen and learn how to prepare and eat it. These are invaluable life lessons, taught in a hands-on, inspiring environment, and the children just love it. I only wish the program had been around when I was at school!

MAMA DURIE'S GARDEN

COOMBABAH, QUEENSLAND

DELICIOUS GARDENS

My mum has been a passionate gardener for as long as I can remember. She is quite possibly the original seed of inspiration for my career, though I admit it took a while to germinate! She is devoted to all things green and growing, so much so that when she moved house nine years ago her first priority was, "What can we do with the garden?"

My brother and I joined forces to do our own "backyard blitz" as a Christmas present for Mama. We turned her garden into a zero-lawn matrix of pathways with beds that were completely planted out with edible and ornamental plants. We also constructed an orchid house, where she grows more than ninety types of orchids.

No sooner had we finished setting up this fabulous productive, yet private, garden for Mum than she turned it into a neighborhood veggie patch. All the local kids come and hang out with "Mama Joy" in her garden, where she proudly cultivates an urban food bowl that supplies 90 percent of what she eats. The birds and bees are constant visitors, too, and I'm convinced her garden pollinates the entire suburb.

Mum composts, she weeds, and she feeds—and it's not just herself and the neighbors, even the local bandicoot gets a meal! She's planted a cluster of cabbages in a corner of the garden, with one that's especially for the little critter. Mum calls this her insurance, as he'll come back to the same cabbage each time, leaving the rest of her harvest intact!

Mum has an incredible understanding of seasonal harvests, and when we speak on the phone it's always fifteen minutes on what's growing in the veggie patch and five minutes about what's going on in the world.

I've watched this garden give Mum so much energy and nutrition—she really is living proof that gardens provide a sense of well-being and balance. She's always laughing, full of energy, and excited about what the next season will bring.

THE PRODUCE FROM
MUM'S GARDEN INCLUDES:

BANANAS

BASIL

BEANS

BEETROOT

BOK CHOY

BROCCOLI

CABBAGES

CAPE GOOSEBERRIES

CAPSICUMS

CARROTS

CAULIFLOWER

CELERY

CHILLIES

CHIVES

CORIANDER

CORN

CUCUMBERS

DILL

FINGER LIMES

FRENCH BEANS

LEMONS

LETTUCES

LIMES

MANDARINS

MINT

ORANGES

OREGANO

PAPAYA

PARSLEY

PASSION-FRUIT

PINK GRAPEFRUIT

POTATOES

PUMPKINS

ROCKET

ROSEMARY

SAGE

SHALLOTS

CHARD

SNOW PEAS

SWEET POTATOES

THYME

TOMATOES

ZUCCHINI

Q&A WITH MAMA DURIE

What are your most successful edible plants?

"Tomatoes are my most successful edibles by far. They grow all year round in this subtropical climate. My compost provides lots of free tomato plants—there are seeds in it from my kitchen scraps, so when I water it plants just spring up everywhere!'

How do you decide what to plant where?

"I rotate different veggies around the beds. If you plant the same crop in the same place all the time the soil becomes depleted of the nutrients that type of plant uses."

What do you love most about this garden?

"I love that Jamie surrounded the back garden with tall tree plantings to give me a sanctuary where I sit, soak up the winter sun, watch birds, and study vegetable growth."

What is your greatest challenge in this garden?

"I don't have enough space for everything I would like to grow, but I do what I can."

How do you protect your crops from pests and disease?

"I grow everything organically, so I only use organic fertilizers, my own homemade compost, and a chilli and garlic spray that I also make myself."

What advice would you give someone growing edibles for the first time?

"My main advice would be that your plants are only as good as your soil. Prepare it well, with lots of compost and manure."

I love hanging out with my gorgeous mum in her garden.
She is still one of my biggest inspirations.

Pathways and raised beds have made
Mum's garden accessible and functional.

WHAT I LOVE ABOUT THIS DESIGN

My brother and I gave Mum the bones of a productive kitchen garden and, through sheer ingenuity, she's made it her own. She's placed a timber boardwalk through the veggie patch, creating narrow pathways that allow her to tend, sow, and harvest her plants. The boardwalk divides the center of the garden into a grid pattern, so it can be explored from many different angles, which I really like. I love the orchid house, too, which connects the main vegetable garden to the house. She has also created a matrix of found wooden branches that acts as a screen to protect the more delicate plants from the harsh summer sun, and on which edibles can grow. She has placed garden seating around the beds, and she spends many hours there contemplating the world and chatting with her friends over cups of tea, while overlooking her glorious greens. Mum's garden also makes the perfect outdoor dining room, because it's close to the kitchen and living room, and it's surrounded by suspended natural works of art.

Mum is pretty haphazard in terms of what she plants in the beds. The structure she has built gives her enough architecture, form, and function to allow her to be as random and carefree as she likes with planting. Through trial and error, Mum has developed a system that not only educates the neighborhood kids, but also works in harmony with some of the local furry natives.

What I love most about my mum's garden is that it really is the living embodiment of my whole "outdoor room" philosophy. It gives you a wonderful feeling of being enveloped in nature—it's intimate and secluded, and you really get the sense that you are in a special place.

YOU COULD DO THIS

Mum used to complain about mowing the lawn every week—how much water and maintenance it required, and the fact that she got nothing out of it except exercise. My brother and I decided to tear out the old lawn, much to Mum's shock, and replace it with a matrix of pathways and raised garden beds that have become her prime source of food and joy. The matrix also offers up different spaces to sit and relax or entertain. You could do this yourself in any traditional garden space. I'm always telling people to plan out their gardens and compartmentalize the different areas to get the maximum usage out of it. If you replace your lawn with a garden that is ornamental, productive, and interactive, your kids, and the planet, will love you for it.

CIRCULAR BEDS

This free-form design of circles is one I'd encourage anyone to copy—it's a really simple way to create generous raised beds, it's low maintenance, and easy to navigate.

The slices of rainwater tank work really well as plant beds. You can buy cut-down corrugated-iron tanks like this from tank and landscape suppliers—just make sure the top edge has been rolled down or encased with a rubber tube as it's razor sharp.

Once you've cleared the area for the garden, work out the location of your plant beds. Circular ones look great and they are easy to work with, plus they allow a more free-flowing root system. The downside is they're not very space efficient, so if your area is small and square, you're best sticking with square or rectangular beds. You will need to install a utility pathway of about 4 feet around your garden beds for access. To work out the scope of a circular plant bed, put a stake at the center of the proposed location, then tie a piece of string as long as the bed's radius to the stake. Keeping the string taut, walk around until you complete a circle. Stake the ground at regular intervals so you end up with a dot-to-dot style circle.

The next thing to consider is how you'll keep hungry critters away from your edibles. A fully enclosed net is a must in more rural areas, but may not be required in an urban area. You might want to put one in for the look of it, though, or to provide a frame for peas, corn, and other vertical crops. You can buy ready-made nets from landscape supply stores or you can get creative and design your own, like we did for this project. If you choose the DIY route and are new to landscape construction, it may be best to speak to a professional before embarking on your net project.

SUCCESS STORIES

Dave Salter

They say that your garden reflects who you are, and Dave Salter's garden is a great example of this. He loves to garden and he loves to eat fresh food. Dave has been nurturing his garden for around forty years, proving that it is possible to transform basic bush sand, over time, into good, fertile soil.

Over the years and season by season, Dave has slowly built up the soil with organic matter to make it the rich growing medium it is today. He has two large compost crates, one for fresh compost straight from the kitchen and the other for a more "mature' compost that he pre-pares for a year in readiness for spring planting. Dave's main challenge is that the garden is on a slope, so water and nutrients are not retained as well as they could be. Increasing the richness of the soil has helped this, as has planting across the slope to create a natural depression. Dave also harvests rainwater, collecting enough to sustain the garden year-round.

Dave's edible plant selection is based on what he enjoys eating and what thrives in his conditions. He loves the tropics, so he's included edible plants that add a tropical flavor, such as coffee, bananas, pineapples and mangoes. As well as producing an abundance of fruit, some of these plants have created subtle design features. Pineapples are a terrific accent plant, for example, due to their dramatic architecture. Any plant with some sort of central spike or flower will make a good accent plant. I use accent plants in my gardens in the same way people use vases in their living room. They draw the eye and provide a great focal point.

Some of Dave's simple growing structures are successful design features, such as the bamboo teepees that support sweet potatoes and beans, and the functional cement footpath that takes you around the garden, under citrus and mango canopies and through an edible wonderland. What Dave loves most is that he can view all of this from his kitchen window!

CHAPTER FIVE

COMMUNITY CONNECTION

A well-designed and productive garden, no matter how big or small, turns a space into a destination. Community gardens are connecting people and communities the world over, enriching the way people live and interact.

WHAT'S IT ALL ABOUT?

Community gardens are sprouting up all around the world in all sorts of places, from vacant blocks and parks to the sides of streets and rooftops. People love them, and when you see one in action you can understand why. They connect neighbors of all ages and backgrounds, and give them the chance to join forces, physically working together, and emotionally connecting—planting, feeding, weeding, and watering for a common gain. When you join a community garden you make friends while you learn how to grow all sorts of edible plants. Research shows that community gardens play a big part in enhancing people's lives as they work together to create healthy and socially sustainable communities. What's not to love?

In the inner city, where backyards are the exception rather than the norm, community gardens give local residents the chance to "green up" their environment, improve their health and well-being, and reduce their food miles. Some really innovative community gardens have been created in urban locations, such as the Wanaqua Family Garden in New York (pages 158-165).

In this chapter, you'll find everything you need to know about joining a community garden, planting on the side of your own street, or even starting a community garden from scratch. The key things to remember are to enlist help, check with your local government before you start, and keep things simple. Recycle, scavenge, and think outside the box when it comes to materials so you can keep the costs low and get the most out of the plot.

FRANK LLOYD WRIGHT

WHO OR WHAT INSPIRES ME?

Frank Lloyd Wright is a huge inspiration for me. As an architect, he addressed social and global issues with a "green" focus long before the rest of the world caught on.

In 1991, the American Institute of Architects named him "the greatest American architect of all time." But what particularly resonates with me is that he took his inspiration from the cycles of nature. He wanted to find the best possible balance between built and natural environments, with one working in harmony with the other. What a beautiful vision—and he made it happen.

In the early 1930s, he and his wife Olgivanna founded an architectural school at Taliesin, Wisconsin, where students would literally "learn by doing." The apprenticeship program he established, the Taliesin Fellowship, offered a learning environment that included not only architecture and construction, but also farming, gardening, and cooking, plus the study of nature, music, art, and dance. The total package.

Producing homegrown organic food for the Taliesin community is still a vital part of the educational experience at the Frank Lloyd Wright School of Architecture. Wright-designed chicken coops, pigpens, and contoured farmland are landmarks on the estate, with natural prairies, orchards, and wetlands surrounding his architectural structures. Architecture and design stand together with nature, just as he hoped they would.

EAGLE STREET ROOFTOP FARM

This is the kind of rooftop garden that designers dream about. Wow! It is located in Brooklyn, New York, and has the most amazing views of the Manhattan skyline across the East River. It was set up in 2009 on top of a flat warehouse roof and is made up of sixteen garden beds, which occupy about 670 square yards. Over thirty types of produce are grown, ranging from eggplants, carrots, and kale to watermelons and radishes, using organic farming practices. Annie Novak, who cofounded the farm, manages it.

To me, this is the quintessential community garden. Not only does it sell produce to local restaurants (delivery is by bicycle), but it holds weekly farmers' markets, hosts workshops on everything from how to start an urban farm to seasonal planting, and runs volunteer programs on Sundays, when locals can flex their green thumbs by planting, harvesting, and watering to their hearts' content. There are chickens, as well as three beehives from which the farm produces its own honey. There's also a compost program in place, which collects contributions from restaurants and volunteers, and all of the watering is done by hand or from retained rainwater. This community garden really has it all.

Just think about it—with the right motivation, the possibilities are endless. I promise, you will never look at a rooftop the same way again!

DOWN AND DIRTY

HOW TO START OR JOIN A COMMUNITY GARDEN

Starting or joining a community garden can be extremely rewarding. It is a great way to connect with like-minded people and learn how to grow your own food.

Joining a community garden is easy. First stop is to ask your local government about what community gardens already exist in your area. They should have contact details and addresses. Or, if you see one in your local area that you want to join, just drop in and say hi—gardeners are a friendly bunch.

Starting a community garden is a little more complicated. Most governments are very supportive of community garden initiatives and will be able to help you. It takes a lot of planning, energy, and commitment—but it is worth it. What better way to give something back to your community, while helping the environment, saving money, and improving your health at the same time? Here are some tips to help you create a successful community garden:

- **Enlist help:** As the name suggests, a community garden is all about community, and it needs many people to succeed. You need to have a strong core group of dedicated gardeners.

- **Do your research:** Contact your local government, and think about how you want to structure your organization, how you will link to local businesses, how you will fund the garden, how decisions will be made, and how you will create a sense of community.

- **Develop a plan of management:** This will help to clarify your aims and show funding groups and landowners how much thought and research has gone into the project.

- **Develop a design:** The design needs to address the group's needs, wants, and desired outcomes. Identify any potential problems by performing a detailed site analysis before you start. You need to understand the garden's aspect, topography, climate, soil type, solar access, existing vegetation, and structures. The design process can be a bit overwhelming, and I suggest you get help from a qualified landscape designer at this stage if possible.

- **Get building:** Organize a series of "working bees" to build the garden beds and prepare the soil for planting.

- **Hit the books:** There is plenty of information, both online and in print, about starting a community garden, so start reading.

TOOLS
HEIRLOOM SEEDS
$4.50 EACH
TOMATO
TOMATO
CHILLI
MARIGOLD
CAPSICUM
CUCUMBER
SWISS CHARD
SPINACH
CABBAGE
CELERIAC
MUSTARD
KOHL RABI
EGG PLANT
LEEK
PEAS
SEEDS

FORAGING

Foraging is simply searching for food in public areas—by the side of the road, near railway tracks, on pavements, or in local parks, woods, and shorelines. It has become so popular in recent years that even restaurants are getting in on the act.

Many plants commonly classified as weeds, such as dandelion, chickweed, and blackberries, are actually useful food and medicinal crops. On Sydney's northern beaches, where I live, I've taken to foraging for a weed known as pennywort. In Sri Lanka it is known as gotu kola and is used in yummy sambals or "mallung," a salad-style accompaniment to a typical curry. This plant is also very good for internal health, stomach ulcers, fever, and asthma and has been used in Ayurvedic medicine for centuries.

There are so many edible plants growing everywhere; foraging is a great way to explore them. Get educated, get enlightened, and get eating!

Common edible weeds

- **Dandelion:** All of the plant is edible. Eat the root raw, roast it for a coffee substitute, put the young leaves and flowers in salads, and braise older, more bitter leaves.
- **Chickweed:** Just about everyone has chickweed in their backyard. Throw it fresh into salads or cook it quickly in a stir-fry. It is high in vitamin C and has been used to aid weight-loss and assist with asthma and allergies.
- **Purslane:** This plant has a slightly salty, sour taste and a crunchy texture, and is great in salads, baking, and soups. It has high levels of omega-3 fatty acids and vitamins A and C. You can also eat the seeds.
- **Nasturtiums:** You can eat the whole plant, which has a peppery, spicy taste. Add it to salads—it is rich in vitamins A, C, and D.

Foraging tips

- The most important rule of foraging is: if you're not 100 percent sure of what it is, don't eat it!
- The best place to start foraging is in your own backyard, which is likely to have lots of weeds. Instead of poisoning or composting them, throw them into a salad and enjoy the local flavor.
- Like any other plants, weeds are seasonal. Do your research so you know what you are looking for and when.
- Avoid foraging on former industrial sites, as wild herbs and weeds soak up heavy metals from the soil.
- Some local governments poison weeds in public spaces, so call your government to check before harvesting.

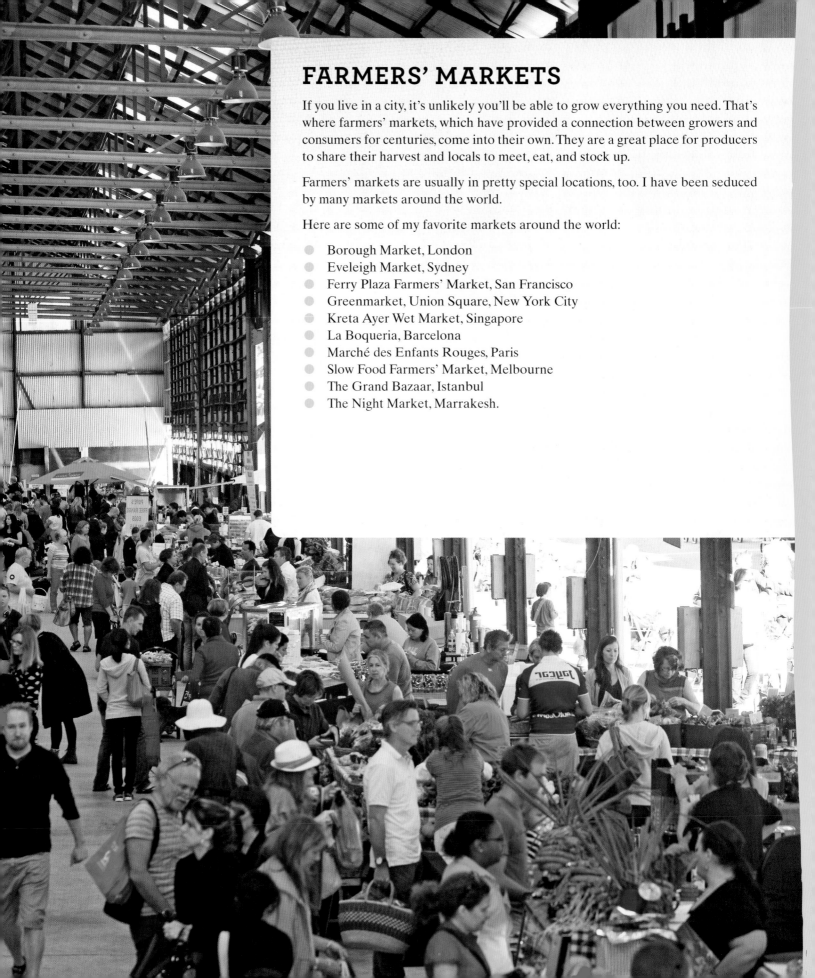

FARMERS' MARKETS

If you live in a city, it's unlikely you'll be able to grow everything you need. That's where farmers' markets, which have provided a connection between growers and consumers for centuries, come into their own. They are a great place for producers to share their harvest and locals to meet, eat, and stock up.

Farmers' markets are usually in pretty special locations, too. I have been seduced by many markets around the world.

Here are some of my favorite markets around the world:

- Borough Market, London
- Eveleigh Market, Sydney
- Ferry Plaza Farmers' Market, San Francisco
- Greenmarket, Union Square, New York City
- Kreta Ayer Wet Market, Singapore
- La Boqueria, Barcelona
- Marché des Enfants Rouges, Paris
- Slow Food Farmers' Market, Melbourne
- The Grand Bazaar, Istanbul
- The Night Market, Marrakesh.

Steve Wheen's little garden creations add some green magic to neglected spaces.

GUERRILLA GARDENING

The aim of the guerrilla gardening movement is to transform neglected or vacant land (public or private) into fertile green space by planting edible or ornamental plants. The guerrilla gardener's weapon of choice is a seed bomb or "green grenade" (see pages 154-155). I have a real soft spot for the guerrilla gardening movement. I love its defiance, its sense of childish innocence and fun, and that it's making a stand for beauty and nature, in the hope that nature will win the day.

Have you heard of the Pothole Gardener? His name is Steve Wheen and he's being hailed as the "Banksy of Guerrilla Gardening." Steve began his guerrilla gardening with magical miniature garden installations in potholes on his street in London because he didn't have a garden. After creating the tiny scenes, he would photograph them and post them on his blog. He has received so much attention he has now published a book, *The Little Book of Little Gardens*.

URBAN AND COMMUNITY GARDENS

In your home

You could build a garden anywhere, from a contemporary urban space to a larger rural area or farm garden. Planters made from concrete pipes will last forever and need zero maintenance to look good. The main thing to be conscious of is how much the pipes weigh. Don't even consider using them on a rooftop or balcony! They are fine for the backyard, but you do need to make sure you have a solid foundation. Get advice from a qualified landscape contractor or structural engineer before you start. And remember, they will need many hands to install!

Alternatively, you could use cardboard tubes for a similar look without the weight. The insides are waxed and the outsides are pressed cardboard. The cardboard is biodegradable, and I love the idea of the tubes slowly decomposing as the plant roots establish themselves in the ground.

In your neighborhood

If you are inspired to create a community garden in your own neighborhood, here are a few tips to help you get started:

- Before you do anything, contact your local government. They will help you understand the relevant guidelines and policies, and may even be able to assist the project through community grants.

- Ask the government for advice about the locations of underground pipes and cables, so that you don't cause any accidental damage to essential services while building your garden.

- If you want to plant edibles in the ground, rather than in raised beds, test your soil first for heavy metals and chemical pollution. Many inner-city suburbs have a history of industrial use, and the soil might be unsuitable or even contaminated.

- Don't forget that your garden is a public space. Expect and encourage interaction from others. This may include growing a little extra produce for street food giveaways.

- Involve your neighbors. Talk to them about their expectations, likes, and dislikes, and make sure that you're all on the same page before launching into your community garden project.

- Get in touch with other people who have built similar community gardens.

SEED LIST

Edible plant seeds
basil
marigold
chives
dill
lettuces
nasturtiums
parsley
sunflower
tomatoes

SEED BOMB RECIPE

"Seed bombs," densely packed balls made up of seed, fertilizer, and potting mix, have been used for centuries as a way of rapidly greening large areas, both urban and rural. Today, guerrilla gardeners toss them over fences to encourage plant growth in urban wastelands.

Seed bombs are not only appealing to mischievous adults, but also a great way to encourage children to get involved in gardening. How can something that involves getting dirty, throwing things, and watching plants grow not appeal to kids?!

Tips

- Use a range of different plant seeds in your bombs; small seeds work best, as they bind to the clay more easily. See the seed list (left) for edible plant seeds you could use.

- Be sensible about the plants you choose. Don't use anything that can become invasive, such as noxious weeds, or anything in the mint family.

- Consider the time of year you plan to bomb, and what plants would be best sown at that time. Spring is a good time for many edibles, including parsley, lettuce, basil, and tomatoes.

Ingredients

- 1 cup potting mix or compost
- 1 cup potter's ball clay (available from craft stores)
- ¼–½ cup edible plant seeds (this is determined by seed size, for example, ½ cup for large seeds, such as sunflower, and ¼ cup for small seeds, such as parsley)
- seaweed solution or water

Method

POTTING MIX
+
CLAY
+
SEEDS

- In a large bowl, mix the potting mix or compost with the clay and seeds until combined.

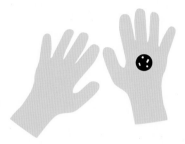

- Add the seaweed solution or water drop by drop to form a dough. Try not to make the balls too wet, or you will end up with a sticky mess!

- Using your hands, roll the dough into balls the size of golf balls.

- Place the balls on a sunny windowsill or in a dehydrator to dry as soon as you have finished making them. This prevents the seeds from germinating in the moist clay and compost mixture.

- Once the bombs are completely dry, put them in a bag, then wander around your backyard or neighborhood and do some bombing!

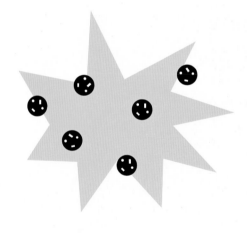

- The bombs will rest on the ground until there is enough rain to break them down so that the seeds can germinate and the plants begin to sprout.

CONTAINER GARDENS

You could easily create a container garden in your own backyard. Two of its main features are the no-dig garden and the use of recycled materials. Here are a few bits of advice about these.

Creating a no-dig garden

I reckon this is one of the greatest garden inventions ever. It's so easy to make—it's just like assembling lasagne, but using layers of organic matter instead! A no-dig garden can be placed on any surface, as long as there is proper drainage. Here's how you do it.

Ingredients

- newspaper or cardboard
- straw or sugarcane mulch
- animal manure (cow, chicken, or sheep) or blood and bone—if you use blood and bone, add 1 part sulphate of potash to 10 parts blood and bone before sprinkling onto the bed
- compost

This list is by no means exhaustive. You could also use mushroom compost, peat moss, or composted vegetable waste. The whole thing should be a mixture of soil (about 40 percent) and organic matter (about 60 percent), built up to a height of at least 16 inches. The most important thing is the balance between carbon (newspaper, straw) and nitrogen (manure, fertilizer), because carbon needs a good supply of nitrogen to help it to break down.

Method

- Build or buy your raised garden bed. You might want to build edging around it to help prevent erosion and nutrient runoff. To maintain good drainage, which is critical, you could place permeable weed matting underneath the mounded earth.
- Start with a layer of newspaper or cardboard, about ¼ to ½ inch thick. This foundation will help to suppress weeds, so make sure there are no gaps. Water it well to help it start breaking down.
- Cover the newspaper with thick wads of straw. Water lightly.
- Add a layer of animal manure or blood and bone.
- Cover the manure with a layer of loose straw.
- Add another layer of manure or blood and bone. Water lightly again. You can create as many layers as you like.
- Once you've finished your layers, add a nice thick layer of compost over the whole surface area.
- When the bed is the right height (at least 16 inches high), I like to finish it off by covering the surface with a mixture of soil (40 percent) and organic matter (60 percent) until it's about 4 inches thick. If you don't have enough compost, create pockets where you will be planting.
- Once your bed is built, wait a week or two for it to begin decomposing. Keep it moist, but not wet.
- The bed will sink as it breaks down, so top it up with animal manure and hay, when necessary.

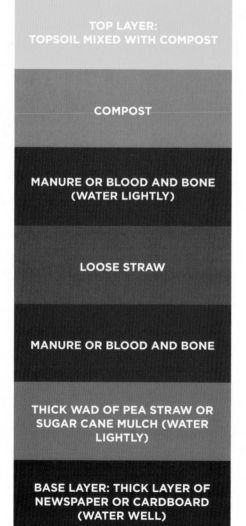

TOP LAYER: TOPSOIL MIXED WITH COMPOST

COMPOST

MANURE OR BLOOD AND BONE (WATER LIGHTLY)

LOOSE STRAW

MANURE OR BLOOD AND BONE

THICK WAD OF PEA STRAW OR SUGAR CANE MULCH (WATER LIGHTLY)

BASE LAYER: THICK LAYER OF NEWSPAPER OR CARDBOARD (WATER WELL)

Recycled materials

I can't urge you strongly enough to use recycled materials in your garden—it's a great way to reduce your carbon footprint. These days you can buy recycled products at most landscape supply stores, or you can have some fun scouting around junk shops and garage sales.

Here are some common garden materials you could replace with recycled alternatives:

- **Gravel:** Crushed gravel is a great foundation, but if you'd like to be a little more green-minded, try crushed recycled concrete. This will reduce the amount of man-made waste going into landfill, which in turn means less stone and gravel that needs to be quarried. Crushed recycled concrete comes in a range of particle sizes and is available from most hardware stores, garden supply centers, and home improvement centers.
- **Timber:** Consider using a recycled plastic composite substitute.
- **Paving:** Many natural stone products come from quarries in developing countries, where there are issues such as child labor, groundwater contamination, and land degradation. Use recycled bricks and stone from your local area if possible.

WANAQUA FAMILY GARDEN

NEW YORK CITY

DELICIOUS GARDENS

Sandwiched between apartment buildings and a public school, this fantastic community garden connects people of all ages and cultures. The site, which is owned by the City of New York, had been vacant for many years and was overflowing with rubbish when locals began transforming it into an urban edible oasis. Soon, with support from GrowNYC, a local nonprofit environmental organization, this unused space became a thriving hub for community gardeners and local schoolkids.

In 2011, Jeff Wandersman of Palette Architects, following extensive community consultation, created a garden master plan. The aim was to come up with a design that would allow the space to be used for education as well as growing food. The garden they designed is divided roughly into thirds. One-third is used as a teaching garden for the schoolkids, one-third is a community garden where locals grow their own produce, and one-third is a central timber pavilion with a kitchen, barbecue, and seating areas, plus an area for tool storage.

The school uses the space as an outdoor classroom, where students can plant their own vegetables and watch them grow, while the community gardeners also use the space for local events.

Another thing that's special about the Wanaqua Family Garden is that it's located in Mott Haven, South Bronx, which is a mainly Latino neighborhood. That cultural heritage is reflected in the plants, the social events, and the way the garden is decorated—flags of many of the gardeners' home countries fly from the central pavilion.

This is one of the many wonderful things about gardening—it can reach across cultural and demographic divides, bringing us all together. To me, it's like music and art—nature has no boundaries and it touches all of us, because we are intrinsically a part of it.

Many hands make light work. A group of like-minded people came together and a community garden was born!

The timber pavilion is the heart of the garden, the magnet that draws everyone to the main gathering place in the middle.

EDIBLES GROWING IN THE WANAQUA FAMILY GARDEN INCLUDE:

BASIL

BEANS

BEETROOT

BROCCOLI

CHIVES

CORIANDER

CORN

EGGPLANT

PEACH

RADISHES

STRAWBERRIES

Q&A WITH JEFF WANDERSMAN

What has been the most surprising element of the garden?
"How well utilized it has become. Many classes are held in the garden every week and the schoolchildren are excited to have an opportunity for hands-on learning. There is a core group of community members who use the garden on a daily basis, tending their plots. The benches and shaded hangout spaces also make it an ideal space for neighborhood parties and barbecues."

What was the greatest challenge when designing and building the garden?
"The project budget and labor force were the most difficult challenges. We could only use off-the-shelf materials, and we couldn't use intensive construction techniques or heavy machinery labor with a limited workforce of GrowNYC staff and volunteers.."

What is your vision for this garden?
"The garden is not yet complete. It continues to evolve with small renovations from the community members, giving it its own unique character. As the community continues to use the garden, we hope the structure and layout will continue to change to make it as personalized and useful as a small piece of open space in a crowded city can be."

WHAT I LOVE ABOUT THIS DESIGN

They say a kitchen is the heart of every home, and this garden really is the heart of its neighborhood; it's wonderful that everyone uses it for celebrations and entertaining. The Wanaqua community and their extended family even hang out here. There are garden beds made from concrete and timber, and there's a communal outdoor dining room slap-bang in the middle of the garden where everyone gathers. All the uses are integrated with this design—people truly live in this garden.

Here are some other features I love:

- **Site design:** Gardening space is maximized, with the pavilion for socializing and educational activities in the center of the garden.
- **Cost-effectiveness:** I admire the resourcefulness of the team at Wanaqua Family Garden, how they've worked with existing materials rather than modifying or manufacturing materials.
- **Construction:** Due to the volunteer workforce, the pavilion had to be easy to build. The architects created a simple structure, using very basic materials, that could be assembled by novice builders.
- **Water storage:** The architects designed an ingenious inverted gable roof with a central drain to divert rainwater into a tank at the rear of the pavilion. The drain is both practical and a striking design feature.
- **Concrete troughs:** I really like the retro feel of the concrete troughs that have been planted with vegetables. They make a nice change from the timber or corrugated steel often used.
- **Kid friendly:** It's great that children growing up in one of the world's most famous concrete jungles have the opportunity to come to a garden like this to learn about growing food and the natural rhythms of nature.

GARDENING WITH CHILDREN

As you can see from the Wanaqua Family Garden, community gardens also make wonderful classrooms. They teach children a wide range of life skills, including:

- **Responsibility:** looking after plants and encouraging their growth
- **Cooperation:** working as part of a team
- **Nutrition:** understanding the food cycle and learning new ways to grow and eat food
- **Respect for nature**
- **Reasoning and scientific inquiry:** they learn about botany, science, and horticulture in a fun environment
- **Imagination:** best of all, kids discover things about themselves when they play in nature. Don't organize every outdoor activity for your kids; it's important to leave them alone to explore and get inspired by themselves. I believe that it was while spending time like this when I was a child that I really got in touch with my imagination and my whole inner world.

YOU COULD DO THIS

The Wanaqua Family Garden is so much more than a veggie patch—by adding seating, shade, and an area for people to congregate, they've created a magnet within their outdoor space that attracts people! Here are some ideas you might want to try in your own local community or school garden to bring together people of different ages and ethnicities:

- Create a rainbow garden reflecting the diversity of your community. Research plants grown and eaten by various ethnic groups and plant them in your garden. Make signs for each plant, including its name, origin, growing, and food preparation tips.
- Start a gardening buddies program, where children are paired with older gardeners from within the community or a local nursing home. This not only ensures that valuable gardening knowledge is passed down through generations, it also provides activity for elderly gardeners.
- Look out for unfamiliar plants at your local food market, read up on how to grow and cook them, then try to grow them yourself.
- To encourage children into the garden, give them their own patch and provide easy-to-grow plants like beans, nasturtiums, strawberries, tomatoes, and corn. Involve them in all the stages of plant growth, from sowing and watering to harvesting and eating. Most importantly, roll up your sleeves and join them. Dig for worms, search for snails, look for ladybirds, teach them how to make mud pies. Let them get down and dirty!

CHAPTER SIX

PERMACULTURE

Permaculture begins with respect—for plants, animals, people, and cultures. From this comes interest, observation, and understanding. By observing how natural ecosystems survive and flourish, we can learn how to apply these natural cycles to our own lives. The result? A more harmonious and sustainable lifestyle.

WHAT'S IT ALL ABOUT?

Permaculture is a holistic method of gardening devised by Bill Mollison and David Holmgren in the 1970s. It involves working as closely as possible with nature, minimizing waste and maximizing symbiotic relationships. What this means is using natural methods to do everything from attracting insects and deterring pests to enriching the soil and creating shade or support. The focus is on creating systems that are both productive and energy-efficient, so you can get the most out of your land with the least amount of effort.

One of the principles of permaculture is to turn problems into solutions. As Bill Mollison once said, "You don't have a snail problem, you have a duck deficiency." This ties in with the science of biomimicry, which involves using natural processes to solve human problems. I really love this approach. When you think about it, almost every challenge we face has been solved already in nature—we just need to look around and find the solution, then work out how to apply it. A good example of this is Velcro, which was modeled on the way burrs stick to dog hair. Genius! There's much to be gained by studying our environment and designing our lives to work with, rather than against, it.

Now, you might think that permaculture is better suited to large gardens, but it can guide the way you manage even the smallest plot. It begins with thoughtful design, including zoning, and companion planting (see pages 172–73). When it comes to choosing plants, look for those with multiple functions, such as screening, dividing, or creating microclimates and producing as well. Animals and insects, such as bees, chickens, goats, and cows, can also be used to help fertilize, pollinate, and control weeds and pests.

What you're aiming to do is create a balanced environment that mimics nature. Setting up a permaculture garden does require a reasonable amount of research and planning, but once everything's in place you're on easy street. Basic maintenance is all that's required—nature will take care of the rest.

WHO OR WHAT INSPIRES ME?

BILL MOLLISON

It's impossible to talk about permaculture without mentioning environmental scientist Bill Mollison. He and David Holmgren created this revolutionary concept, then proceeded to spread the word. In fact, two of my team have completed their programs and both came away committed to growing their own food in a natural and sustainable way.

Born and bred in Tasmania, Bill spent many years working on the land and at sea, including wildlife and marine research, and this opened his eyes to the devastating effect humans are having on the environment. His Eureka moment came when he realized we should be working with nature, rather than against it, applying our knowledge of ecology and physics to our own environment. This means that gardens, however large or small, should be designed as self-contained ecosystems that require minimal maintenance for maximum production.

Bill believes that permaculture is a concept everyone can grasp—it's a common sense approach to creating an environment in harmony with nature. There's no complicated technology or special machinery—just careful planning, so the design conforms to the land. Plants and animals are chosen for their suitability to the site—climate, location, soil, and so on. It's gentle and sustainable, and a great way to set up an edible garden.

"PERMACULTURE... A PHILOSOPHY OF WORKING WITH, RATHER THAN AGAINST, NATURE; OF PROTRACTED AND THOUGHTFUL OBSERVATION, RATHER THAN PROTRACTED AND THOUGHTLESS LABOR; AND OF LOOKING AT PLANTS AND ANIMALS IN ALL THEIR FUNCTIONS, RATHER THAN TREATING ANY AREA AS A SINGLE-PRODUCT SYSTEM."

-BILL MOLLISON

BEEKEEPING

Did you know that for every three mouthfuls of food we eat, one can be linked directly to the work of bees? These amazing little creatures pollinate many of our edible favorites like tomatoes, onions, stone fruits, carrots, and beans. In Europe and North America, urban beekeeping is enjoying a surge in popularity due to concerns over severely declining honeybee populations. Without them, many food crops can't be pollinated, so it's a serious problem.

You might also be surprised to hear that bees make great pets. Sure, they're not as cuddly and friendly as dogs and cats, but they're relatively low-maintenance and incredibly useful, pollinating plants and producing honey. They're pretty cute, too!

If you'd like to install some beehives in your backyard, learn as much as you can about beekeeping by taking a course, joining your local beekeeping club, and talking to professional beekeepers. Once you've got the know-how, you can think about the how-to. There are two ways to keep bees. The first is DIY—you invest in the hives, equipment, and bees, and manage them yourself. The second is to host hives owned by a professional beekeeper—you get the bees without the responsibility, and it's a low-commitment way to see if beekeeping works for you.

Beekeeping checklist

Before you commit to any hives, make sure you've considered the following:

- **Location:** Bees need a protected, dry, sunny position close to an accessible water source.

- **Flight paths:** Bees are busy creatures, and at times there will be lots of them buzzing to and from the hive. Make sure you understand their flight paths and keep them as far away as possible from areas people use often. Increasing the height of the fence around the hive may encourage them to fly above head height.

- **Legalities:** Legal requirements regarding beekeeping vary. For information about regulations in your area, contact your local government.

- **Neighbors:** Some people suffer from a life-threatening bee allergy and others may have a fear of bees, so make sure you talk to your neighbors and be clear about your intentions. Offering them the odd pot of honey may help sweeten the deal!

"IF THE BEE DISAPPEARED OFF THE FACE OF THE EARTH, MAN WOULD ONLY HAVE FOUR YEARS LEFT TO LIVE. NO MORE BEES, NO MORE POLLINATION ... NO MORE MEN."

-ALBERT EINSTEIN

COMPANION PLANTING

Picture your garden as a community. Plants are supposed to grow together so they can help one another along the way, whether through diversification, attracting beneficial insects, deterring pests, enriching the soil, or creating shade or support. For example, poppies attract hover flies, which are beneficial insects. Spend time observing and understanding your garden's unique habitat, and through trial and error you will discover what teams work in your environment.

HERE ARE SOME
TRIED AND TESTED
COMPANIONS THAT
WILL HELP A VARIETY
OF EDIBLE PLANTS

TOMATOES · CUCUMBER
MARIGOLD
LETTUCE AND MOST PLANTS

Benefit
Repels white fly and root
knot nematodes.

SPINACH · SWISS CHARD
CORN
LEAFY GREENS

Benefit
Protects and shades delicate
leaves from harsh sun.

STRAWBERRIES · CUCUMBER
BORAGE
MOST EDIBLE PLANTS

Benefit
Increases yield by adding nitrogen
to the soil and attracts bees.

FRUIT TREES · TOMATOES
ONIONS AND GARLIC
EGGPLANT

Benefit
Help deter aphids, slugs, and
other insects and weeds.

GRAPES · TOMATOES
GERANIUM
EGGPLANT

Benefit
Attract insect pests so they
stay away from other plants.

TOMATOES · BERRIES
COMFREY
FRUIT TREES

Benefit
The leaves are full of nitrogen,
phosphorus, and potassium.

CABBAGE · RADISHES
NASTURTIUMS
APPLE TREES

Benefit
Attract aphids so the aphids
avoid other plants.

CABBAGE · CARROTS
SAGE
STRAWBERRIES

Benefit
Repels the cabbage
white butterfly.

SEED SAVING

Seed saving is about more than just growing good vegetables inexpensively. It's also about preserving biodiversity, culture, and history, and ensuring food security.

In the old days, farmers would save seeds each year and this would gradually alter the genetic makeup of the crop to suit the growing conditions. These days, big companies control much of the seed market and most of our edible plants come from just a few highly developed varieties. These hybridized seeds have some advantages, such as bigger fruit, better cold/heat tolerance, and ease of harvest, but there are some serious downsides. When they are planted exclusively, the genetic diversity of older plant varieties is lost, and we become dependent on external suppliers to provide seeds for us.

Genetic diversity helps plants adapt to a changing world. Just say you put in a crop of hybridized tomatoes and it was attacked by a pest or disease. All the plants would probably be affected, because hybridized seeds have a small gene pool. But if you had planted an heirloom crop, you'd find that some of the plants would be more resilient than others. Seed saving is a bit like a plant insurance policy—it avoids you putting all your eggs in one basket (see page 184 for more about seeds and how important their preservation is for the future).

Another reason to save seeds is that if you harvest them from your star performers and sow them the following year, you're developing a line of plants that should thrive in your particular garden. Gardeners have been doing this for thousands of years—now it's your turn to contribute to the story.

Seed-saving tips

- There are two methods for saving seeds (see diagram on facing page). Use the dry method for edibles such as beans, broccoli, cabbage, carrots, carrots, cauliflower, corn, herbs, leeks, lettuce, onions, peas, and most flowers. Use the wet method for seeds from fleshy edibles such as cucumbers, melons, pumpkins, squash, tomatoes, and zucchinis.

- Only save seeds from non-hybrid plants, as they're the most likely to produce plants that closely resemble their parents. These seeds are usually referred to as open-pollinated, heritage, or heirloom seeds.

- Save seeds from your best fruit and vegetables, and eat the rest.

- Harvest seeds at the end of the season, once the fruit and the seed have fully matured. Seeds collected from a plant whose fruit hasn't ripened will not germinate. The seeds are ready to harvest once the flowers fade and dry. Edibles with pods should be brown and dried out.

HOW TO SAVE SEEDS

- Choose which of your plants you want to keep growing.

- Harvest your seeds from the healthiest, most mature plants at the end of the season.

EXTRACT
+
CLEAN SEEDS

- Use the dry or wet method, depending on the chosen plant (see Seed-saving tips, opposite).

Dry method

- The seed heads need to be completely dry. If they are not completely dry when picked, put them in a paper bag to dry.

- Separate the seeds from the seed heads.

- Winnow the seeds by placing them in a bowl or sieve and gently shaking in a circular motion.

Wet method

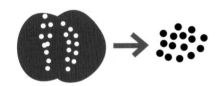

- Cut the fruit or vegetable open and extract the seeds.

- Put the seeds in a sieve and wash with a blast of tepid water.

- Dry the cleaned seeds completely on a sheet of newspaper.

- Store the seeds in a labeled, sealed paper bag or envelope.

SUCCESS STORIES

Michele Margolis

Michele Margolis started getting serious about her own edible utopia about twenty years ago. She had three young children and was keen to go back to nature with their food consumption. Michele started with a selection of edible plants that she and her family enjoyed eating and were suitable for her climate and growing conditions, and then designed the garden following the principles of permaculture. I think she's really got it right.

Michele has created a productive and sustainable urban backyard that runs entirely on rainwater. With about fifty fruit trees (including coffee, mango, limes, lemons, macadamia, avocado, and bananas) and hundreds of herbs and vegetables, it provides a great variety of food throughout the year. Michele's garden really sums up the three ethics of permaculture design: care of the earth, care of people, and fair share.

Michele has also created a thriving local permaculture community of like-minded people. They focus on building food security, enriching the soil with organic matter for local community gardens, recycling urban waste, raising bees, establishing a local eco-library and seed library, and encouraging others to learn about and live a seed-to-plate existence. "It's a connection that needs to happen for us to value food, farmers, and caring for our soil," says Michele.

Local bee expert Gavin Smith supplies the network with hives and also brings Michele trailer-loads of food waste from local markets to turn into seasonal preserves, feed her chickens, and to help build up the local soil supply with organic matter.

"Becoming a beekeeper has changed how I feel about the garden. It offers a sense of connectedness. The pleasure is in the learning journey—the less I know, the more there is to learn and that is as true with bees as it is with plants."

CHAPTER SEVEN
AN EDIBLE FUTURE

All around the world, people are embracing the desire for a more local and sustainable existence. Kitchen gardens, backyard chicken coops and beehives, recycled materials, and compost bins are all back in style. Innovative gardening methods, such as vertical growing, permaculture, and aquaponics, are making sustainable living possible in urban areas. Edible gardens are the way of the future, and now's the time to jump on board.

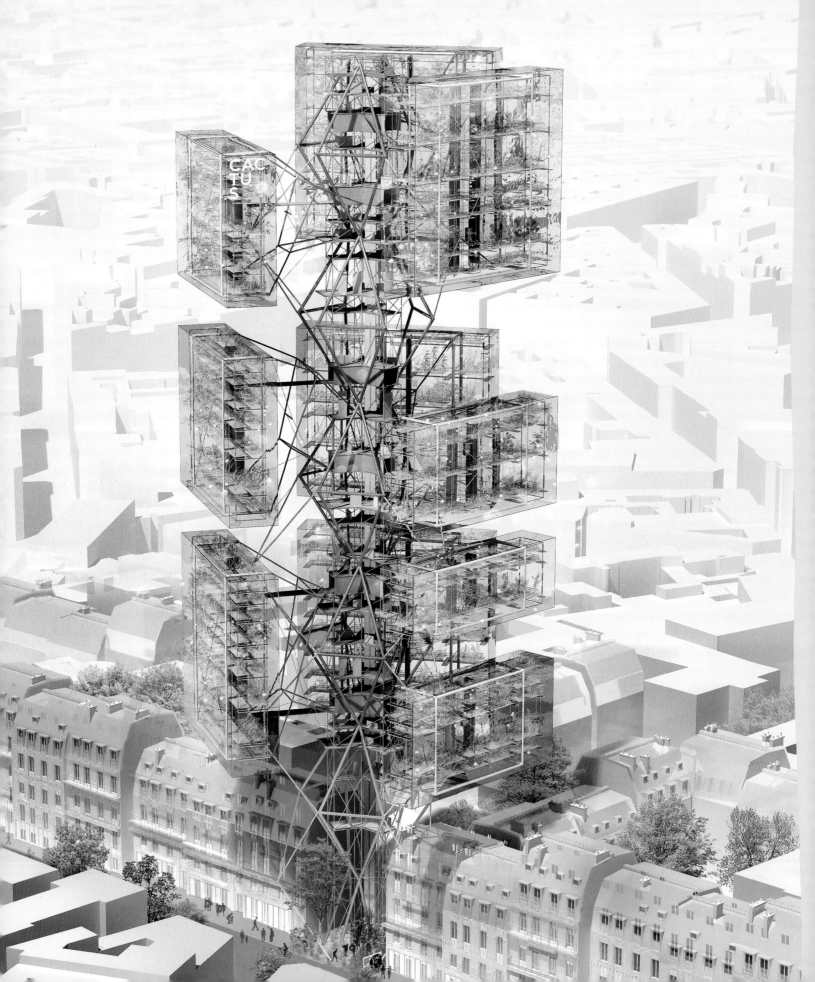

WHAT'S IN STORE?

INNOVATION

Interest, imagination, and innovation are what make the future of edible gardening so exciting. More and more people are starting to grow their own food and take an interest in where it comes from, and it's sparking their imagination. We have seen really innovative use of recycled materials and brilliant space-saving ideas. Meanwhile, environmental scientists and experienced gardeners are devising clever, contemporary solutions for edible gardening, especially in urban areas, such as vertical gardens (chapter 3) and aquaponics (pages 186-187). All these innovations are bringing our food closer to home—reducing food miles and prices, and improving quality and freshness. Rooftop gardens, greenhouses, and community gardens are sprouting up all over the world in countries with densely populated urban centers, such as Japan, China, France, and the United States.

"Building up" to maximize both green space and overall living space is one of those design solutions that's so practical and straightforward, it's hard to believe we didn't think of it earlier. But with our ever-increasing population and the resulting issues of urban sprawl, now is certainly the time to get into it. Vertical gardening allows us to grow gardens anywhere, on an apartment balcony, in a small backyard, even up the side of a multistory building in the heart of the city. In these urban environments, vertical gardens offer a breath of fresh air—literally, because they generate oxygen, cleaning the air around them, and creating mini-ecosystems where airflow is recycled. There are already seven operational vertical farms (that's right—farms!) in the world, in Japan, Korea, Singapore, the Netherlands, Sweden, the United States, and Canada, and more are on the way.

Something we did think of many years ago, and which is enjoying a popular revival, is the greenhouse. It's been the savior of gardeners and farmers in cold climates for centuries, and contemporary greenhouses are still based on the original design. Greenhouses are now being utilized in remote areas (such as Lille Fro, pages 54-57) and urban communities (such as Roppongi Nouen Farm in Tokyo, page 58), extending the growing season so food can be produced well into the cold winter months.

EDUCATION

Teaching the next generation about growing food, good nutrition, sustainability, and a healthy lifestyle is a huge priority, and it's wonderful to see so many organizations and individuals leading the charge. From kitchen garden programs to community gardens, from restaurants with kitchen gardens to people growing edibles in their own backyards, this grassroots movement will shape the way we feed ourselves in the future. Eating food direct from the source, whether it's your own garden or a friend's, a farmers' market or a community garden, is much more satisfying on so many levels.

An amazing educational resource that's often overlooked is botanic gardens. There are over 1500 of these throughout the world and I'd strongly encourage you to visit as many as you can. They're beautiful places to explore and many offer guided talks and programs about a wide range of topics. The New York Botanical Garden is a standout in my mind. This vibrant city does museums and galleries so well, and its botanical garden is equally impressive. As well as being a stunning destination to explore at any time of year (made all the more impressive by its location, slap-bang in the middle of one of the most populous cities in the world), it offers a range of interactive programs, including The Edible Academy. The Academy runs a program for children from preschool age through to high school; professional development classes for teachers; and interactive programming for families. All the programs are hands-on, with the goal of teaching children how to grow fruit and vegetables, and make the connection between plants, gardening, nutrition, and a healthy lifestyle. These are life lessons I think every child should learn.

KITCHEN GARDEN PROGRAMS MAKING A DIFFERENCE

- The Edible Schoolyard Project, Berkeley, California
- GrowNYC, New York City
- Growing Chefs, New York City
- The White House Kitchen Garden, Washington, DC
- Jamie Oliver's Kitchen Garden Project, United Kingdom
- GrowingGreat, California

"IF YOU THINK IN TERMS OF A YEAR, PLANT A SEED; IF IN TERMS OF TEN YEARS, PLANT TREES; IF IN TERMS OF 100 YEARS, TEACH THE PEOPLE."

– CONFUCIUS

KEW MILLENNIUM SEED BANK

Plants are essential for our survival, so preserving seeds for future generations is really important. Collecting, researching, and storing native seeds helps ensure the knowledge and functions contained in plant DNA aren't lost forever. Mother Nature is still the ultimate source of nutrition and natural medicines! Right now, almost a quarter of all the plant species in the world are facing the threat of extinction, so time is of the essence. The Kew Millennium Seed Bank, located in the United Kingdom, is a world leader in seed preservation.

Dr. Tim Entwisle is the Director of Conservation, Living Collections and Estates at the Millennium Seed Bank. He is not only responsible for the priceless stockpile of seeds and the critical science to both test and use it, but he also looks after the vast plant collections growing in Kew Gardens and Wakehurst Place. It's a huge job, but enormously rewarding. "Every one of the more than 30,000 different species that are represented in the seed bank will have some role to play in the livelihood of humans or other animals," says Entwisle. "As an example, ten new species of edible yam have been discovered in Madagascar, including *Dioscorea orangeana* in 2009. Kew has a permanent field base in Madagascar and has discovered, described, and 'banked' hundreds of plant species on the island, including these yams. *Dioscorea organeana* is restricted to an area of less than 5 square kilometers and has been heavily exploited already for food. Kew scientists are working with local communities to conserve and grow the plant sustainably, including the creation of demonstration plots to encourage use of high-yielding cultivars, rather than the endangered wild species. An expedition is also being mounted to secure enough seed for the Millennium Seed Bank, which already holds thirteen of the forty species endemic to Madagascar."

What is Dr. Tim Entwisle's vision for the future of the seed bank and the future of food?

"The first decade of the Millennium Seed Bank was all about numbers, getting 10 percent of the world's flora banked by 2010. We are well on the way to our next target of 25 percent of the world's bankable seeds by 2020, but that's only part of the story. We are moving from a savings bank to an investment bank. A good example is the Crop Wild Relatives project, where we are working with other seed banks and research groups to identify and store species related to those we depend on for agriculture, so that we can breed and propagate varieties to combat climate change, drought, and plant disease. If humans are to survive and thrive on planet Earth, we need the ability to adapt to a changing environment, and a seed bank, with associated research and expertise, will be essential."

WHO OR WHAT INSPIRES ME?

"THE KEW MILLENNIUM SEED BANK PROJECT IS PERHAPS THE MOST IMPORTANT CONSERVATION INITIATIVE EVER."
—DAVID ATTENBOROUGH

"PLANTS ARE ALSO VITAL FOR MEDICINE. ABOUT 70 PERCENT OF THE WORLD'S POPULATION RELIES ON TRADITIONAL PLANT REMEDIES FOR MEDICINE. ONLY ONE IN FIVE PLANT SPECIES HAS BEEN SCREENED FOR USE IN MEDICINE. CURES FOR DISEASES COULD LIE IN MANY OF THESE UNSCREENED SPECIES."

—DR. TIM ENTWISLE

DR. VANDANA SHIVA

Physicist, philosopher, and environmental activist Dr. Vandana Shiva is the powerhouse behind the preservation of seeds globally from a grassroots level. In 1991, she founded Navdanya (meaning "nine seeds"), an organization whose aim is to protect nature and people's rights to biodiversity, water, food, and local knowledge. It does this by starting community seed banks to work toward a more sustainable existence. Set up in rural India, Navdanya is showing the world how to put the power of food back into the hands of the individual and local community.

Dr. Shiva believes that organic farmers are the true scientists of today, as they have to understand how nature and natural cycles work together to produce food. They are not just farmers, she says, but also health specialists, ecologists, and peacemakers.

"THE WORLD HAS TO BE FED. IT HAS TO BE FED BY GROWING FOOD LOCALLY, TO BE USED LOCALLY."

— DR. VANDANA SHIVA

AQUAPONICS

Aquaponics is a combination of hydroponics and aquaculture that is designed to mimic a natural river system. Fish and plants are raised in an integrated system, where the plants rely on the fish for nutrients and the fish rely on the plants for water filtration. It is a closed-loop system, which means the plants and fish don't rely on external inputs for survival (with the exception of fish food). The results speak for themselves—aquaponic plants often grow four times faster than those in a soil garden, but need only 10 percent of the water.

Aquaponics basically works like this: the fish produce waste that is pumped through a biofilter, where good bacteria convert the ammonia and nitrites into nitrates, which is a nutrient for plants. The nitrate-rich waste water is then fed to plants growing in hydroponic beds. The plants clean the water by absorbing the nitrates in it, then it is returned to the fish and the cycle begins again.

If you care enough about your health and nutrition to grow organic edible plants, it's worth considering aquaponics because it's a highly efficient system, thanks to the nutrient-rich pond water. Almost every herb, vegetable, and fruit plant can be grown really successfully this way, from citrus right through to mushrooms.

There is a range of aquaponic systems available for backyard farmers, from highly engineered and complex ones to simple set-ups with just a pond and a pump. Once established, they're pretty easy to run, but it's worth talking to an expert about the type of system that is best suited to your space, climate, and lifestyle.

Things to consider:

- **Placement:** Don't forget that most edible plants prefer full sun, while fish prefer shade and a stable temperature.

- **Maintenance:** Simple aquaponic systems are pretty low maintenance. Once they're established, the only maintenance required is cleaning the pump, tank, and grow beds occasionally, plus testing the pH and nutrient levels when you increase the number of fish.

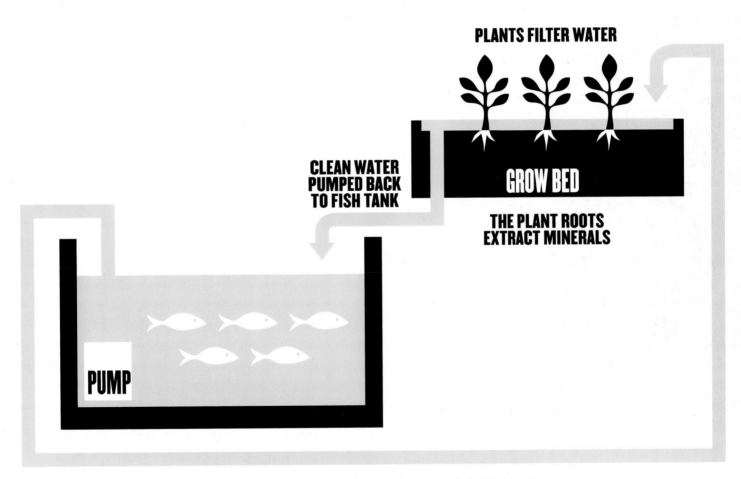

PLANTS FILTER WATER

GROW BED

CLEAN WATER
PUMPED BACK
TO FISH TANK

THE PLANT ROOTS
EXTRACT MINERALS

PUMP

MINERAL-RICH WATER PUMPED TO GROW BED

THE PLANT
CHICAGO

DELICIOUS GARDENS

If urban food production is the way of the future, The Plant, "a net-zero energy vertical farm" at a former meatpacking plant in downtown Chicago, is leading the charge. With its vast indoor facilities, aquaponic growing systems, and rooftop gardens, The Plant takes urban farming to a whole new level. The project is still in its infancy, but when finished it will operate completely off the grid, powered by a renewable-energy system that uses food waste to supply all its heating and power needs.

Farming takes up one-third of the space at The Plant, and the other two-thirds is used for sustainable food businesses. It aims to be a closed-loop system, meaning that the different operations within the building will use each other's waste products to ensure minimal inputs and outputs. For example, spent grains from the brewery at The Plant will be fed to the aquaponic fish; the fish waste will provide nutrients for mushroom crops; and mushroom compost will be used to invigorate vegetable growth.

One of the businesses housed within The Plant is The Urban Canopy. Its goal is to illustrate how rooftop farming can create a sustainable food system in urban areas. Alex Poltorak, the business owner, is passionate about providing fresh produce to local communities in an organic, sustainable, and equitable way. The Urban Canopy's garden has been designed to illustrate the benefits of growing food in the city.

The Urban Canopy team has created beehives from found timber, given coffee sacks a new lease of life by growing potatoes in them, and adapted pickle buckets discarded by fast-food restaurants for the hydroponic system. It's a dumpster diver's paradise!

Food from The Urban Canopy is sold to subscribers via Community Supported Agriculture (CSA). People pay for a share of the anticipated harvest and receive a box of produce each week. Alex says, "This makes planning and budgeting easier and more consistent, as well as cutting out a lot of non-value-add steps in the typical supply chain. Since our farm is tiny and we wanted to highlight urban agriculture in general, we put products from other businesses in The Plant into our CSA boxes, too."

EDIBLES GROWN AT
THE PLANT INCLUDE:

CHOCOLATE MINT

CROOKNECK SQUASH

LEMON CUCUMBERS

NOSEGAY PEPPER

OKRA

ROUND ZUCCHINI

TOMATOES 'GARDEN PEACH'

WHEATGRASS

Q&A WITH ALEX POLTORAK

What is your favorite plant in the garden?
"All the plants we grow work together to create a diverse and healthy ecosystem, but if I had to choose a favorite, I'd say tomatoes. We have forty varieties!"

What feature materials did you use in the garden, and why?
"Anyone can find everything we used in the garden in their local area, either from a recycling center, hardware store, or dumpster. We incorporated used coffee bags from the local roaster, lumber pieces from surrounding construction sites, bamboo shafts, and other secondhand materials. We also created all our own soil and fertilizer from composted food scraps and wood chips."

What is your vision for this garden?
"The farm aims to show how idle rooftops, vacant lots, and empty buildings can all be part of creating a sustainable and equitable food system. Imagine a future where each neighborhood has multiple community gardens, rooftop farms, and indoor growing spaces where we produce much of our fresh food, compost much of our waste, and employ our neighbours—that's our vision." It's my vision, too, Alex . . . of utopia!

WHAT I LOVE ABOUT THIS DESIGN

What's not to love? It's ambitious, innovative, and clever—everything has a purpose and contributes to a greater good.

The Urban Canopy has shown great initiative and resourcefulness by using plumbing pipe to create a forest of tree-like structures that looks like installation art, but is actually a high-tech vertical farm.

I really like the way they have used composted food scraps and wood chips to create their soil. It's more complicated than buying it, but it'll be much more rich and fertile, and converting waste materials into a valuable garden resource is something we could all do a lot more. We need more people like Alex Poltorak on this planet if we want to make the most of every growing opportunity.

The inclusion of an aquaponics system at The Plant is just the icing on the cake for me.

YOU COULD DO THIS

The vertical garden towers at The Urban Canopy would work well in any edible garden, but are particularly suited to a rooftop or balcony, or any awkward space. Here, they are set up in a hydroponic growing system, with a central reservoir to catch rainwater and pump it into the top of each tower. After being used to water the plants, the water is recycled back to the reservoir, ensuring no wastage of water or nutrients.

You can pick up plumbing pipes from any hardware or plumbing supply shop. If you'd like to use a rainwater tank or reservoir to water the plants, you'll just need to install a pump and switch to get the water to the plants. If you're not sure how to go about it, ask a licensed plumber or irrigation contractor to help you set up the pump system.

If you'd like to venture down the aquaponics route (see pages 186-187), it's best to talk to an expert about a system that will suit your space, location, needs, and budget.

I love the clever way Alex has used plumbing pipes to create a unique innovative vertical garden.

SUCCESS STORIES

The Lee family

This basic backyard aquaponic system for a family of five is a great example of how to integrate aquaponics into your space. Aquaponics expert and designer Charles Bacon converted a previously unused part of the garden into a productive hub of herbs, veggies, and fish. The system consists of a pond for the fish, a pump, and four grow beds for plants and filtration. Water is pumped from the fish pond to the grow beds and returned, filtered, using gravity.

The grow beds, built from railway ties, are placed in full sun, which is ideal for edible plants. Gravel is used in the grow beds and a bell siphon regulates the water, flooding and draining the beds at intervals to provide oxygen for the plant roots and bacteria. The sunken pond is in a shaded corner, providing a stable temperature for the seventy-five silver perch, with a cascade for aeration.

GROW A BETTER FUTURE

> "TO FORGET HOW TO DIG THE EARTH AND TEND THE SOIL IS TO FORGET OURSELVES."
>
> —MAHATMA GANDHI

> "BY CONNECTING WITH PLANTS AND WILDLIFE, WE CONNECT MORE DEEPLY WITH ALL OF NATURE: OUR ENVIRONMENT, OUR HOME, OUR FAMILY, AND, ULTIMATELY, OURSELVES. THIS, IN THE END, IS WHAT LIFE'S ALL ABOUT."
>
> —JAMIE

GROWING TRENDS

- Vertical gardens and farms to maximize our living and growing spaces, especially in urban areas.

- Greenhouses to extend growing seasons and create microclimates in harsh climates.

- Utilizing unused urban spaces, including rooftops, vacant lots, and streetscapes to grow edibles.

- Alternative growing methods, including aquaponics and hydroponics.

- Establishing community partnerships and encouraging small-scale farming.

- Localizing food production to reduce food miles.

With world population growth now outweighing our ability to produce food for everyone, we really have no alternative but to become more self-sufficient and expand farming into private gardens. This places less impact on the world's farms and puts the power back in our own hands—the power to nurture our family and friends with good nutrition.

You can grow a better future by planting a garden you can eat. It's as simple as that, however, I want you to do it with thoughtful design. Design your outdoor room and landscape it the same way you normally would, but think outside the square by using food plants instead of, or in combination with, non-food plants. In no time at all, this approach will become a habit. When you're searching for a screening plant at the local nursery, instead of choosing a bamboo or cypress, you'll go for an edible alternative such as a pineapple guava or pomegranate. Instead of softening a paved area in the garden by planting seaside daisies, you'll put in some apple mint or oregano. You'll be swept up in the joy of true earth-to-table living. Guaranteed.

The information in this book is just the tip of the iceberg lettuce! There are so many edible alternatives to the plants you may be used to landscaping with right now. Edible landscaping is a rapidly growing movement around the world and this book highlights just a handful of its heroes.

I sell a range of seeds and the edible ones far outsell the flower varieties. It isn't just a fashion fad either, this food revolution is really happening, a back-to-basics change in mainstream values that is having a wonderful social impact and providing a more hopeful future for our children. The big difference between the kitchen gardens of years gone by and those of today is that we live among our edibles now; they've been integrated into our outdoor lifestyle. The edible garden has finally come of age.

JAMIE'S TOP FIVE TIPS FOR SUSTAINABLE LIVING

RECYCLE AND REUSE
EVERYTHING FROM WATER TO SCRAP METAL. THIS WILL CUT DOWN ON WASTE, ENCOURAGE INNOVATION, AND IMPROVE NATURAL LIFE CYCLES.

THINK SUSTAINABLY
SAVE SEEDS, SAVE WATER, REDUCE ELECTRICITY, AND USE NATURAL PEST SOLUTIONS.

GROW YOUR OWN FOOD
EVEN IF YOU START WITH JUST ONE PLANT. WHATEVER YOU CAN'T GROW, BUY LOCALLY.

CREATE A LOCAL COMMUNITY
YOUR NEIGHBORS, FAMILY, WORK COLLEAGUES, OR A LARGER COMMUNITY— SO YOU CAN EXCHANGE IDEAS, NURTURE, AND SHARE.

REDUCE FOOD WASTE
COMPOST, FREEZE, OR BUY LESS TO START WITH.

MOVERS & SHAKERS

Alice Waters
Chez Panisse & The Edible Schoolyard Project
1517 Shattuck Avenue
Berkeley, CA 94709
chezpanisse.com
+1 510 548 5525
edibleschoolyard.org
+1 510 843 3811

The Cooperative Food Empowerment Directive
cofed.coop
2150 Allston Way
Suite 400
Berkeley, CA 94704
info@cofed.coop

Eagle Street Rooftop Farm, New York
rooftopfarms.org
44 Eagle Street, Greenpoint,
Brooklyn, NY 11222

The Edible Academy – New York Botanical Garden
nybg.org/education/edible-academy
The New York Botanical Garden
2900 Southern Boulevard
Bronx, NY 10458
+1 718 817 8700

Edible Green Wall – Atlanta Botanical Garden
atlantabotanicalgarden.org
1345 Piedmont Avenue NE
Atlanta, GA 30309
+1 404 876 5859

The Edible Schoolyard Berkeley
edibleschoolyard.org/berkeley
Martin Luther King Jr Middle School
1781 Rose Street
Berkeley, CA 94703
+1 510 558 1335

Esther Deans' Gardening Book: Growing without Digging
by Esther Deans
(Harper & Row, 1977)

Ferry Plaza Farmers' Market, San Francisco
ferrybuildingmarketplace.com/farmers_market.php
Ferry Building Marketplace
One Ferry Building
San Francisco, California 94111
+1 415 291 3276

Frank Lloyd Wright Foundation
franklloydwright.org
info@franklloydwright.org
+1 608 588 7090

Frank Lloyd Wright/ Taliesin Fellowship School of Architecture
taliesinpreservation.org
taliesin.edu
tours@taliesinpreservation.org

The Garden at Stonefields
by Paul Bangay and Simon Griffiths
(Lantern Penguin, 2013)
paulbangay.com

Geoffrey Bawa
geoffreybawa.com

Greenmarket, Union Square, New York
grownyc.org/greenmarket
GrowNYC
51 Chambers Street, Room 228
New York, NY 10007
+1 212 788 7476

Grow City – Edible Rooftop Gardening
grow-city.org

Growing Chefs, New York
growingchefs.org
annie@growingchefs.org

Growing Great, California
growinggreat.org
2711 North Sepulveda Boulevard #279
Manhattan Beach, CA 90266
info@growinggreat.org
+1 310 939 9216

GrowNYC, New York
grownyc.org
51 Chambers Street, Room 228
New York, NY 10007
+1 212 788 7900

Guerrilla Gardening
guerrillagardening.org
richard@guerrillagardening.org

Jamie Durie
jamiedurie.com
Level 2, 9 Waratah Street
Mona Vale, NSW 2103
+61 2 9998 8900
8033 Sunset Boulevard #427
Los Angeles, CA 90046
+1 323 654 2206
feedback@jamiedurie.com

DURIE□**DESIGN**

Jamie Durie Design
jamieduriedesign.com
studio@jamieduriedesign.com

Jamie Oliver's Kitchen Garden Project
jamieoliver.com/kitchen-garden-project/
19–21 Nile Street, London N1 7LL
kitchengarden@
jamieoliverfoundation.org

***The Last Child In The Woods:
Saving our Children from
Nature-deficit Disorder***
by Richard Louv
(Algonquin Books, 2008)
richardlouv.com

The Little Book of Little Gardens
by Steve Wheen
(Dokument Press, 2012)
thepotholegardener.com

Modern Sprout, Chicago
modernsproutplanter.com
sprout@modsprout.com

***The Nature Principle: Reconnecting
with Life in a Virtual Age***
by Richard Louv
(Algonquin Books, 2012)
richardlouv.com

Patio by Jamie Durie
bigw.com.au/jamie-durie
+1 800 244 999

Patrick Blanc
verticalgardenpatrickblanc.com
contact@patrickblanc.com

The Plant, Chicago
plantchicago.com
1400 West 46th Street
Chicago, IL 60609
info@plantchicago.com
+1 773 847 5523

Planting Justice
plantingjustice.org
996B 62nd Street
Oakland, CA 94608
+1 510 290 4049

The Pothole Gardener
thepotholegardener.com
thepotholegardener@yahoo.com

The Reality of Food Aid
by Bill Pritchard
tedxsydney.com/site/item.cfm?item
=6DC220E4C290F6C97F0E31D1E9
1EFBBD

Riverpark Farm, New York
riverparkfarm.com
450 East 29th Street
New York, NY 10016
info@riverparkfarm.com

Slow Food USA
slowfoodusa.org
68 Summit Street, 2B
Brooklyn, NY 11231
+1 718 260 8000

**The Spotted Pig, New York
(April Bloomfield)**
thespottedpig.com
314 West 11th Street
New York, NY 10014
+1 212 620 0393

Terrain
shopterrain.com
561 Post Road East
Westport, CT 06880
914 Baltimore Pike
Glen Mills, PA 19342
service@shopterrain.com
+1 877 583 7724

**The Urban Canopy, Chicago
(Alex Poltorak)**
theurbancanopy.org
|poltorak.alex@gmail.com

**The Urban Homestead, Pasadena
(Dervaes family)**
urbanhomestead.org
631 Cypress Avenue, Pasadena, CA
91103-2905
info@urbanhomestead.org
+1 626 795 8400

***The Vertical Farm: Feeding
the World in the 21st Century***
by Dickson Despommier
(Picador, 2011)
verticalfarm.com

**Wanaqua Family Garden, New York
(Palette Architects)**
grownyc.org/openspace/gardens/
bx/wanaqua
460-464 East 136th Street
Mott Haven, Bronx, NY 10454

**The White House Kitchen Garden,
Washington DC**
whitehouse.gov/interactive-tour/
kitchen-garden
The White House
1600 Pennsylvania Avenue NW
Washington, DC 20500
+1 202 456 7041

Windowfarms
windowfarms.com

PICTURE CREDITS

Page 115: left image © Rick Chapman; right image © Jiri Hera/Shutterstock.

Pages 116–117: Tonya McCahon © JPD Media + Design.

Page 118–119: Jason Busch © JPD Media + Design.

Page 120–121: apples 'Crimson Crisp', broad beans and lettuce 'Italian Lollo' © Simon Griffiths; blackcurrants © Igor Normann/Shutterstock; broccoli © Emily Goodwin/Shutterstock; carrots 'St Valery' © Natursports/Shutterstock; celeriac ©Dimitrios/Shutterstock ; figs 'Black Genoa' © Ratikova/Shutterstock; heirloom tomatoes © blanche/ Shutterstock; plums 'Santa Rosa' © Vezzani Phototgraphy/Shutterstock; pomegranates © Arakelyan Andrey/ Shutterstock; potatoes 'Royal Blue' and 'Dutch Cream' © Sompoch Tangthai/ Shutterstock; raspberries © topseller/ Shutterstock; redcurrants © Loskutnikov/ Shutterstock; rhubarb 'Wandin Giant' and 'Ever Red' © mikeledray/Shutterstock; strawberries 'Red Gauntlet' © Martin Kubat/Shutterstock.

Page 122–125: Jason Busch © JPD Media + Design.

Page 126: bananas, beans, beetroot and bok choy © Simon Griffiths; basil © Jan Havlicek/Shutterstock; broccoli © Emily Goodwin/Shutterstock; cabbages © silver-john/Shutterstock; cape gooseberries © InavanHateren/ Shutterstock; capsicums © Denis and Yulia Pogostins/Shutterstock; carrots © Albert Michael Cutri/Shutterstock; cauliflower © turtix/shutterstock; celery © Angela Andrews/Shutterstock; chillies © inchich/Shutterstock; coriander © freya-photographer/Shutterstock; chives, mandarins and parsley © Jamie Durie; corn © lola1960/Shutterstock; cucumbers © John Goldstein/Shutterstock; dill © freya-photographer/Shutterstock; shallots © Vlad Ageshin/Shutterstock; finger limes © Glenn Price/Shutterstock; french beans © Lissandra Melo/Shutterstock; lemons © studiogi/Shutterstock; lettuces, mint, oregano, rosemary and sage by Jason Busch © JPD Media + Design; limes © S. Bonaime/Shutterstock; mint by Jason Busch © JPD Media + Design; oranges © Irina Fischer/Shutterstock; papaya © antoni halim/Shutterstock; passionfruit © matin/Shutterstock; pink grapefruit © Radu Bercan/Shutterstock; potatoes © Sompoch Tangthai/Shutterstock; pumpkins © Malgorzata Litkowska/Shutterstock; rocket © Planner/Shutterstock; silverbeet © Krishnadas/Shutterstock; snow peas © JIANG HONGYAN/Shutterstock; sweet potatoes © Jackiso/Shutterstock; thyme © Diana Taliun/Shutterstock; tomatoes © blanche/Shutterstock; zucchini © Sfocato/Shutterstock.

Pages 127–131: Jason Busch © JPD Media + Design.

Pages 132–133: Jason Busch © JPD Media + Design.

Pages 134–135: © Jason Busch © JPD Media + Design.

Page 136: © Jason Busch.

Page 138: Jason Busch © JPD Media + Design.

Page 140: © John Engstead.

Page 141: © Caroline Hamblen.

Pages 142–143: Tonya McCahon © JPD Media + Design.

Pages 145–146: Jason Busch © JPD Media + Design.

Page 147: © Christian Jung/Shutterstock.

Pages 148–149: Jason Busch © JPD Media + Design.

Pages 150–151: © Steve Wheen.

Pages 152–153: Jason Busch © JPD Media + Design.

Page 154: Tonya McCahon © JPD Media + Design.

Page 155: illustration by Evi O © Penguin Group (Australia).

Pages 156–157: Jason Busch © JPD Media + Design.

Pages 159–161: Tonya McCahon © JPD Media + Design.

Page 162: basil © Jan Havlicek/Shutterstock; beans and beetroot © Simon Griffiths; broccoli © Emily Goodwin/Shutterstock; chives © Jamie Durie; coriander © freya-photographer/Shutterstock; corn © lola1960/Shutterstock; eggplant © Denis and Yulia Pogostins/Shutterstock; peaches © Iryna1/Shutterstock; radishes © Olha Afanasieva/Shutterstock; strawberries by Jason Busch © JPD Media + Design.

Pages 163–165: Tonya McCahon © JPD Media + Design.

Page 168: Jason Busch © JPD Media + Design.

Page 170: © Lisa Mollison.

Page 171: © irin-k/Shutterstock.

Page 172: Jason Busch © JPD Media + Design.

Page 173: illustration by Daniel New and Evi O © Penguin Group (Australia).

Page 174: Tonya McCahon © JPD Media + Design

Page 175: illustration by Evi O © Penguin Group (Australia).

Pages 176–177: Jason Busch © JPD Media + Design.

Page 178: © Jason Busch.

Page 180: illustration © SOA Architects.

Pages 182–183: Tonya McCahon © JPD Media + Design.

Page 185: top image © The Millennium Seed Bank, Wakehurst Place; bottom image by Jason Busch © JPD Media + Design.

Page 186: Jason Busch © JPD Media + Design.

Page 187: illustration by Evi O © Penguin Group (Australia).

Page 189: Tonya McCahon © JPD Media + Design.

Page 190: chocolate mint © 336food/ Shutterstock; crookneck squash © islavicek/Shutterstock; lemon cucumbers by Tonya McCahon © JPD Media + Design; nosegay pepper © JPD Media + Design; okra © infocus/Shutterstock; round zucchini © Elliotte Rusty Harold/ Shutterstock; tomatoes 'Garden Peach' © AN NGUYEN/Shutterstock; wheatgrass by Tonya McCahon © JPD Media + Design.

Page 191–193: Tonya McCahon © JPD Media + Design.

Page 194–195: Jason Busch © JPD Media + Design.

Page 202: Jason Busch © JPD Media + Design.

Design of chapter openers and plant list templates inspired by Florence Broadhurst wallpapers, courtesy of Signature Prints, Sydney, Australia.
signatureprints.com.au

ACKNOWLEDGMENTS

A huge thanks to Didee Mitton for project managing all aspects of this project and putting up with my crazy schedule, and to Georgie Reid for her support on the "Delicious Gardens" case studies in the book.

My gratitude also to Jason Busch, Tonya McCahon, Andrew Curtis, and my dear friend James Houston for all their wonderful photography and for pulling together the material, no matter the season. Thanks to Allyson Ireland from Beautiful Spaces Inside & Out and Mark & Louella Tuckey for providing us with wonderful props. Also, thanks to all the talented and dedicated people who allowed us to include their fantastic, inspiring gardens in this book. It's all of you and your yummy gardens that inspired me to write this book and feature your extraordinary contributions: Alice Waters, Stephanie Alexander, Lille Fro, Roppongi Nouen Farm, The Spotted Pig, Sibella Court, Riverpark Farm, the Kershaw family, Patrick Blanc, Samantha & Seth Barnes, Cromer Community Center, Flower Power, the Dervaes family, the Paperbark Camp team, Dave Salter, the Wanaqua Family Garden, Annie Novak & Eagle Street Rooftop Farm, Steve Wheen, the Valder family, David Holmgren, Michele Margolis, New York Botanical Garden, Dr. Tim Entwisle, Dr. Vandana Shiva, The Plant Chicago, the Lee family, Tamara Cannon, Frank Lloyd Wright Foundation, John Engstead, Caroline Hamblen, Rick Chapman, Atlanta Botanical Garden, Bill & Lisa Mollison, Charles Bacon, GrowNYC, Eveleigh Market, New York Greenmarket, Bar H, Kent Bangay, and Dickson Despommier.

Thank you, Helen and David Lennie from Signature Prints for allowing me to replicate some of the great Florence Broadhurst designs with edibles.

Thanks to my amazing team at Durie Design and JPD Media, especially my rock, our creative director Nadine Bush—I'd be lost without you. Thank you too to Emma Paling, Andrew Pawsey, Tim Bradshaw, Desmond Stock, and Paulina Frankowski for their input.

To the entire Penguin team, you are all so talented. The incredible powerhouse, Julie Gibbs, Katrina O'Brien, Nicole Abadee, Evi Oetomo, Daniel New, Alison Cowan, Anna Scobie, Rachel Carter, and Tracey Jarrett for all their support, dedication, and hard work in making this book as lush and beautiful as it could possibly be.

Lastly, I would like to thank my mother, Joy, for instilling in me a passion for gardening and the natural world. A huge thanks to all my friends and family for their continued love and support.

INDEX

Jamie Durie OAM is a horticulturalist, award-winning landscape designer, product designer, and the author of nine bestselling books, including *Patio*, *The Outdoor Room*, *Outdoor Kids*, and *100 Gardens*. He founded *The Outdoor Room* magazine and has hosted more than fifty television shows worldwide, including *Top Design*, and made regular appearances on the *Oprah Winfrey Show*. He is also the creator of *The Outdoor Room* series, which airs in more than twenty countries.

Jamie has been creating gardens since 1998, and has thirty-three international design awards to his credit. These include gold medals at the Chelsea Flower Show and numerous other garden shows across the Asia Pacific region, as well as a Centenary Medal and Medal of the Order of Australia for his services to the community and the environment. He is the founder and principal designer of Durie Design, with offices in Sydney and Los Angeles, and his work spans thirteen countries.

When he's not working, you'll find Jamie in his favorite place . . . the garden.

JAMIEDURIE.com

JAMIEDURIEDESIGN.com